BaltSe@nior - Challenges and innovative solutions in product development for seniors' home living

Edited by Elina Priedulena and Beata Fabisiak

Published by

Baltic Sea Academy e. V.

Dr. Max A. Hogeforster

Blankeneser Landstrasse 7

22587 Hamburg, Germany

Editorial Correspondence: editor@baltic-sea-academy.eu

Printed by: **BoD-Books on Demand, Norderstedt, Germany**

ISBN 9783749456093

The project BaltSe@nioR has been co-financed by the European Union (European Regional Development Fund) within the INTERREG Baltic Sea Region. This publication does not necessarily reflect the opinion of the European Commission.

Content

Foreword

The ageing of nations observed worldwide is an enormous challenge for governments and national economies as well as for researchers and companies. Above all, it is a challenge for us – the citizens of the Baltic Sea Region (BSR), who are or will be older people – who care for our loved ones in old age and would like to offer them the best care, comfort and security they deserve. Efforts to improve the quality of life of older BSR citizens can give power to our furniture SMEs. As part of the BaltSe@nioR project, experts from all Baltic Sea countries – Poland, Denmark, Latvia, Finland, Lithuania, Estonia, Norway, Germany and Sweden – have therefore developed, tested and made available to SMEs

- ICT based tools, applications and databases;
- innovative, creative working methods, developed in a translational environment and cross-sectional specialization, for product design and development;
- valuable, rare knowledge on, among other things, furniture safety, reliability, specific needs and preferences of seniors, and the problems they face.

In addition, they all worked together on synergies between the traditional furniture industry and innovative ICT solutions, on strengthening the innovation capacity to develop intelligent products adapted to the needs of older people, and on improving the inspiration and common identity of SMEs in the furniture sector, making them and the whole BSR more innovative and competitive.

The contributions in the book include an excerpt of the work from the 3-year project BaltSe@nioR. For further information you are invited to visit the project page: https://baltsenior.com/.

1 | About the project BaltSe@nioR

Beata Fabisiak, Department of Furniture Design, Faculty of Wood Technology, Poznan University of Life Sciences

Elina Priedulena, Hanse Parlament

Challenge to be addressed

The Baltic Sea Region (BSR) faces the huge societal challenge of aging nations. Helping seniors and improving their quality of life is an urgent task and a great market potential for enterprises in the Baltic Sea region. Europe had 90 million of elderly aged 60+ in 2015 (18% of the population). The predictions indicate that the percentage of seniors in European society will reach 24% in 2030 (EUROSTAT). The number of seniors is rising in all continents. By 2050, 2 billion worldwide will be 60+. This enormous challenge can be turned into a great business opportunity since seniors need age-appropriate furniture and interior design enhancing their comfort of living, safety and independence. For many years the problem of aging of societies was unnoticed and neglected. The market offer of products adapted to seniors' needs is fragmentary, or almost non-existent. The previous research (performed within the StarDust project) confirmed that more than 90% of Polish seniors reported not having kitchen adapted to their needs. At the same time, the research proved that seniors make expenditures on furniture, as the majority of them (74%) had bought at least 1 item in the last 5 years. This situation is due to the fact that for many years seniors were not treated as valuable customers having purchasing power. But the times have changed, and also the senior population has transformed. The generation of baby boomers – people born in the period of 1946-1964 – are now entering senior age. This generation has different purchasing behaviour and a different lifestyle than the previous one. Companies need to recognise that in order to capture the market niche.

The furniture industry in the Baltic Sea Region is developing five times faster than in other regions of the EU. The Baltic Sea Region is rich in design traditions and industry potential, with Germany and Poland being the 3rd and 6th biggest furniture producers and 2nd and 4th biggest exporters of furniture in the world. The woodworking industry consists of 1.5 million employees solely in Poland and Germany. World Intellectual Property Organization confirms: in 2013 there were over 207 thousand BSR IP filings in Industrial Design registered, with Germany, Poland and Sweden accounting for 86% of it. In the last decade a huge increase (69%) of that number has been observed in the whole BSR, being over 90% in Poland, Latvia, Estonia and Lithuania. Aspirations to improve life quality of older BSR citizens can actually give even more power to the furniture SMEs.

However, to seize the new demand opportunity (stemming from the needs of aging society), the BSR furniture industry needs support in branding, transnational cooperation and cross-sectional specialization, new product development methods based on a design thinking approach and open innovation, and knowledge on inter alia senior preferences, their home space requirements, etc., to respond optimally to silver economy market changes. Moreover, it is important to point out the lack of EU Standards on Safety Requirements for Furniture for seniors.

There is a great chance for BSR enterprises for raising their competitiveness and innovativeness by being aware of and reacting fast to the new needs and niche that appear not only on the European market but also worldwide.

Another huge challenge is to provide BSR companies insight into new potential markets, and both new working methods and knowledge to develop new products, strengthening their competitiveness and innovativeness and increasing market share and at the same time to assure the society will benefit through smart solutions that enhance independence for the user. This will mean stronger, more innovative and competitive BSR, with higher seniors' life quality, less expenses on healthcare in municipalities, and senior users will gain independence and autonomy and finally good comfort and safety of home living.

To support this process and make BSR stronger, partners in the BaltSe@nioR project, empowered with the broad competencies of leading BSR actors in the field of furniture, design, technology, ICT and robotics, economy and social sciences have developed solutions: databases, innovative, creative working methods for product design and development, and valuable, rare knowledge on, among other things, furniture safety, reliability, specific needs and preferences of seniors, the problems they face when using furniture, etc. Moreover, synergies have been developed between traditional furniture industry and innovative ICT solutions in the process of cross-sectional specialization and encouraging examples of smart furniture supporting seniors in their daily lives have been developed. BSR furniture companies gained inspiration and common identity, enriched with the wise and beautiful story of mystical old oaks. Through the tools and activities organized within the project, knowledge and competences of BSR companies as well as their capability of working in a transnational environment have been enhanced. Consequently, this supported the improvement of their capacity of innovation to create smart products adapted to senior needs, making them and the whole BSR more innovative and competitive.

Objectives and activities

The project BaltSe@nioR was co-financed by the European Union (European Regional Development Fund) within the INTERREG Baltic Sea Region programme under the programme-specific objective: Non-technological innovation: To advance the Baltic Sea Region performance in non-technological innovation based on increased capacity of innovation actors. The project ran from 2016 to 2019.

According to the programme's specific objective, the project had two comprehensive project objectives, but before they are presented, the project's target group should be identified: companies with ambitions to produce home furniture that improve the quality of life, comfort and safety of the elderly. The project's two objectives are:

1. To provide Baltic Sea Region enterprises having ambitions to produce home furniture, improving seniors life quality, comfort and safety, with adequate tools (e.g. knowledge databases, virtual library, web applications), new knowledge (on furniture safety requirements and reliability, ergonomics, elderly people preferences and needs,

the problems they face when using different types of home furniture, etc.) and new working methods (e.g. design thinking, open innovation) for new product design and development to be able to create smart products adapted to senior needs, as well as to enable their application in design and production practice, making them and the BSR more innovative and competitive.

2. To provide Baltic Sea Region enterprises having ambitions to produce home furniture, improving seniors' life quality, comfort and safety, with adequate tools (virtual library with portfolios of designers, companies and students from BSR countries, knowledge databases), new knowledge (on elderly people's households' characteristics in different BSR countries, seniors' preferences and needs in different BSR countries) and new working methods (introduced in the form of Innovation Camp and transnational workshops), new collaboration and learning possibilities for new product design and development to increase their capacity to create smart products adapted to senior needs, making them and the BSR more innovative and competitive.

To achieve all the project objectives the partnership was composed of 10 partners and 6 associated partners from 9 BSR countries. The whole project work was structured in 5 work packages (WPs) containing a considerable number of activities and learning workshops and events.

The presentation of the project will be made following the structure of the project, namely through a short description of the work packages.

Work Package 1: Project Management and Administration

The objective of the work package was to secure the overall project and time management, and to combine and use the resources in the most effective way for benefit of all participants.

1. Project Coordination: The project coordinator was supported by a project team of experts/researchers working together within the previous StarDust project of the BSR programme, but also with experience in leading and participating in a number of other national and international projects. The cooperation between the project partners

has always included management of actions performed by different actors: research institutions, companies and clusters and has been characterised by a high level of innovation, which has proven its worth in a number of patent applications.

2. The decision-making process was made by a Steering Committee comprised of representatives of partner organizations involved meaning: universities, clusters, and municipalities. The Steering Committee had the role of providing strategic level input and decisions related to project activities, securing project support in BSR countries and ensuring engagement from national participants. An Advisory Management Committee was comprised of the project coordinator and the project managers and leaders of work packages and WP activities leaders – researchers, cluster managers. Its aim was the operative coordination of activities and ensuring integration across WPs.

By including partners from all participating countries in the project, the transnational level was ensured both at the decision making and executive level of the project management as well as in supportive structures.

Beyond that, the project had a content management team that was organized by the lead partner who should provide full administrative assistance for the project implementation and a team of financial managers and accountants with the knowledge, skills and experience in various EU programmes which ensured proper project financial management.

Work Package 2: Development of tools to support furniture companies

The aim of the work package was to provide new tools and new knowledge that are transferred to enterprises, thus constituting the key factor in competing on external markets and making BSR more competitive and innovative; to create together the best and most effective ways to communicate and share knowledge manufacturers need in the design process; to provide knowledge necessary and crucial for creating innovative pieces of furniture adapted to elderly people's needs characterized by ergonomics, safety and reliability. The aim was to develop solutions that could help to increase the competitiveness of manufacturers of furniture for seniors, so that they could become leaders in this niche of the market. Due to the project activities the companies are provided with a catalogue of ICT-based tools to improve their innovation capacity and develop intelligent products for older people. All the tools, materials and information are now stored in a BaltSe@nioR Virtual Library (www.baltsenior.com), where anyone interested can join, search for information, instruments, business partners, experts designs, etc. and upload their own valuable content and share it with others. The Virtual Library is the first website based on expert knowledge dedicated to the subject of designing for the elderly. The Virtual Library publishes the results of research carried out as part of the project, as well as a comprehensive bibliography of experts dealing with issues related to the needs of the elderly, the purchasing power of seniors, housing conditions of the elderly, the design process, universal design, robotics, biomechanics, etc. All materials that are uploaded in the Virtual Library are available to its users free of charge.

The work package was divided into the following groups of activities:

2.1 Elderly users-oriented research

2.2 Furniture and companies-oriented research

2.3 Virtual library development

Work Package 3: Development of working methods for new product design

This work package aimed at developing and providing new working methods for product design, using the design approach, open innovation, and the continuous learning and design process with overarching specialisation in art, design, furniture, ICT, robotics, engineering and economics; to stimulate, motivate and facilitate continuous learning across countries and disciplines. In our partnership these competences were located in different BSR countries; thus the transnational character, especially in the development phase, was ensured. The numerous design workshops of transnational character stimulated the cooperation between partners, being a good opportunity to discover the features of work in multinational teams of designers and engineers working together on the subject of designing for seniors, to share experiences and lessons learned. These were the next steps in recognizing the methods that can be used in the process of designing for seniors. Various methods were tested during a series of workshops involving various groups: researchers, companies, students proceeding the process of developing of training methods and programmes for furniture companies.

During BaltSe@nioR project implementation the participants of the workshops were introduced to and also tried to work with various methods and tools: e.g. Basadur, Design thinking method cards, Business Model Canvas, Virtual Room, Virtual Library, User involved design, and information about seniors, sustainability, etc. During the workshops days they used the knowledge and tools in real life during the product and business development process and the results were product suggestions to enhance elderly people's autonomy and wellbeing in their own home.

The aim was also to raise awareness among managers, designers and furniture constructors concerning requirements of the successful process of designing for seniors but also the needs seniors have and how to design products to fulfil them.

A further objective was to improve the capacity of the units by developing innovative products adapted to the needs of older people and using new instruments to gain competitive advantages and strengthen BSR.

The work package was divided into the following groups of activities:

3.1 Innovation Camp and other transnational workshops

3.2 International internships for students

3.3 Business exchange for BSR companies

Work Package 4: Furniture and ICT

This work package was designed to create new breakthroughs using continuous learning and design processes, involving transnational and multidisciplinary experts/researchers/practitioners representing various disciplines: design, wood technology, robotics, biomechanics, welfare technology. Moreover, the aim was to develop individual ICT-based products, each solving an important user problem and having a high market potential. Within this work package we developed the prototypes of smart furniture and interior design elements. They visibly present the possibilities of ICT implementation in furniture for seniors. These are fall detection and the mobile robot, the Smart Mirror and a pressure sensing chair to be used as a controller in activation games and a Smart Chair helping in rehabilitation of seniors. We also introduced the idea and first prototypes of 3D printed handles for furniture adjusted to the changing shape of the human hand and problems seniors face with seizing. All of these constitute inspirational case studies supporting companies in designing smart furniture for seniors. Due to this valuable demonstration action we show that integration of new technologies into traditional furniture is possible and encourages the furniture industry to take that step forward. This can lead BSR companies to gain competitive advantage and start to be leaders implementing new trends on the furniture market and supporting creation of the digital society.

In the listed innovation activities, techniques of rapid prototyping, 3D scanning, 3D modelling and 3D printing have been used. The idea was to search for innovative new product concepts between the boundaries of different scientific disciplines in the multicultural environment of the BSR countries and to use and adapt existing ICT solutions to develop new furniture and other interior elements.

The work package was divided into the following groups of activities:

4.1 Furniture with integrated ICT solutions development

4.2 Pilot design of ICT adjustable kitchen

Work Package 5: Testing

This work package was important to validate the solutions developed during the project implementation: knowledge databases and ICT-based tools from companies and furniture and other types of furnishing elements from end users aged 60 and over. The activities in this work package addressed the issue of furniture safety for the elderly. As previously mentioned, there is a lack of European standards for senior furniture concerning the safety of its use, so the aim was to develop a proposal for such a standard for the testing of furniture concerning the safety of its use and standards concerning the functional characteristics (including dimensions) of home furniture for the elderly. This is of crucial importance as the group of elderly users consists of a large group of people with different disabilities, reduced mobility, cognitive impairment and special needs. Building on this, the intention was to develop a common BSR identity in the form of the furniture safety label, which should be awarded to those pieces of furniture that receive a positive rating according to the developed requirements. The marketing concept and the storytelling material were prepared and enriched with the photographic documentation that enterprises can use in their marketing activities.

The work package was divided into the following groups of activities:

5.1 Furniture for seniors testing standards development

5.2 New tools, solutions, methods testing

5.3 End-user testing

5.4 Furniture safety label development

Project Partnership

The project partners came from 9 BSR countries - Estonia, Latvia, Lithuania, Poland, Germany, Denmark, Sweden, Finland and Norway – creating a network of leading European institutions in various fields crucial for the successful implementation of the BaltSe@nioR project. Altogether the partners have many years of experience in working in different constellations, with innovative methods including end-users, researchers, students and companies.

The partnership:

Poznan University of Life Sciences, Poland

Development Centre UMT Denmark

Art Academy of Latvia, Latvia

Ukmergė District Municipality Administration, Lithuania

Tallinn University of Technology, Estonia

Technical University of Munich, Germany

University of Skövde, Sweden

Hanseatic Parliament, Germany

Satakunta University of Applied Sciences, Finland

Norwegian University of Science and Technology, Norway

Associated Organizations:

Free and Hanseatic City of Hamburg

Business department and furniture cluster initiative at Tibro Municipality

Riga Chair factory

Architect Office Juha Lehto

Lidköping Municipality

Poznan University of Medical Sciences

Poznan University of Life Sciences took the lead of the project. To be stronger in the ICT the leading European players in the field were invited to join the partnership: the Technical University of Munich (TUM) with its Center for Interior for Independent Living, Satakunta University of Applied Sciences (SAMK), Norwegian University of Science and Technology. Strengthening the application of the results in SMEs, the Hanse Parlament – an association and network of 50 chambers of commerce, industry and crafts – came on board. Free and Hanseatic City of Hamburg, Lidköping Municipality and Tibro Municipality supported the project consortium as Associate

Organizations. Clusters, universities, companies and universities, authorities brought in broad competences and specializations. Each partner had its own role and contributed with its core competencies as an expert for: furniture and wood technology – Poznan University of Life Sciences; economy, marketing and branding – University of Skövde; design – Art Academy of Latvia; technology – Tallinn University of Technology; ICT – Satakunta University of Applied Sciences, Norwegian University of Science and Technology; robotics and engineering – Technical University Munich.

With partners who have previously worked together, the launching of the project cooperation was shorter and mutual understanding made it easier to achieve the expected results. The lead partner is a leading scientific unit providing knowledge and education in a wide range of subjects connected with furniture industry. It represents a unique combination of design and engineering skills, with the focus on ergonomics, construction and technology of furniture. It has experience in managing and participating in numerous international and national projects that successfully transfer innovation to the furniture industry, which is reflected in the number of patents already obtained. Development Centre UMT uses innovative methods of cooperation with companies to facilitate the transfer of knowledge to SMEs in the fields of furniture, innovation and design, new materials and sustainability. It has a gold label for Cluster Management Excellence from the European Cluster Excellence Initiative. Art Academy of Latvia (AAL) supports creative collaboration, teaches design thinking in the Baltic States, works with industry, governments and ageing communities to shape the future of longevity. Its major task is to provide three cycle higher education in arts in compliance with the Bologna process. AAL facilitates creativity in Latvia and internationally, thus securing art continuity. AAL offers opportunities for deep and profound studies of art, audio-visual media, and design and art history offered by fourteen departments arranged in five faculties. The Art Academy is a member of various international organizations and has bilateral agreements with more than 121 partnership universities in Europe and beyond. The Ukmergė District Municipality is a municipality in Vilnius County in Lithuania. With the population of around 50 000 citizens it faces a huge challenge concerning the aging process of the society. The authorities being conscious of the situation have been supporting the process of the recognition of the needs of seniors as well as the prototypes' testing phase. Tallinn University of technology is the flagship of Estonian technology education with the Multidisciplinary Design and Engineering programme and offers an excellent combination of technical and design skills. Industrial commitment is represented by companies and clusters to ensure exploitation of results. Technical University of Munich (TUM) is one of Europe's top universities and is committed to excellence in research and teaching, interdisciplinary education and the active promotion of promising young scientists. The Chair of Building Realization and Robotics at TUM is specialized in the field of advanced construction and building technologies as well as Ambient/Active Assisted Living (AAL). Prof. Thomas Bock and his researchers apply their knowledge to develop smart robotic solutions for intelligent living environments to contribute to the demographic challenges of our society. University of Skövde participated with its School of Business. It is one of five schools at this University. It provides modern programmes based on internationally recognized research within Enterprises for the future (EFF). Education and research are done with quality as it's guiding principle, in close collaboration with the surrounding community. The School aims to provide a stimulating and creative environment for both staff and students. Satakunta University of Applied Sciences is a multidisciplinary and international higher education institute on the west coast of Finland. SAMK is a significant creator of experts as well as a developer, a propeller of internationalisation and a promoter of entrepreneurship. The Department of Neuromedicine and Movement Science, at the Norwegian University of Science and Technology, includes study programmes in Physiotherapy, Occupational therapy, Audiology, Human movement science, Activity and health, Elite sports and Health technology. The BaltSe@nioR project is integrated in the GEMS research group where we conduct research into the causes and characteristics of movement disorders, and interventions to improve mobility under various medical conditions.

With our partnership we covered the entire BSR as the challenge we address is essential for the entire region. We believe that the achievement of project objectives was possible thanks to the consortium that was strong and fully equipped with the necessary and complementary competencies.

2 | Upholstered furniture for senior users – analysis of functional solutions

Beata Fabisiak, Robert Kłos, Department of Furniture Design, Faculty of Wood Technology, Poznan University of Life Sciences

The demographic changes occurring worldwide have led to great interest in the subject of designing for seniors. Due to the constantly increasing number of seniors in modern societies, designers, companies and researchers face a great social and economic challenge. The predictions of the United Nations (2015) state that global ageing will accelerate in the coming decades. In the year 2015 over 900 million people (12% of the global population) were 60+, but it is estimated that by 2050 seniors will comprise 22% of the world population (i.e. over 2 billion persons). This is due to the projected overall reduction in fertility and the growing rate of population ageing worldwide (United Nations, 2015). Nowadays Europe is the oldest region of the world, with 24% of the population aged 60+ (He et al., 2016).

Table 1 presents the increase in the number of older adults in various countries of the Baltic Sea Region in the years 1976-2016. It is worth noting that in all analysed BSR countries the percentage of older population in society was at a similar level. In 2016 Poland was characterized by the lowest proportion of seniors in society. However, according to the Polish Central Statistical Office, the percentage of people aged 60+ in 2050 is to increase to 40.4%, which will correspond to 13.7 million people (Fig. 1).

Table 1. Percentage of people aged 65+ in the country population

Country	Year		
	1976	**1996**	**2016**
Denmark	13.5	15.1	18.8
Finland	10.8	14.3	20.5

Germany	14.6	15.6	21.1
Lithuania	11.2	10.3	19.0
Poland	-	11.2	16.0
Sweden	15.2	17.5	19.8
Estonia	12.4	13.7	19.0
Latvia	12.8	13.8	19.6

Source: Own calculations based on Eurostat data 2017

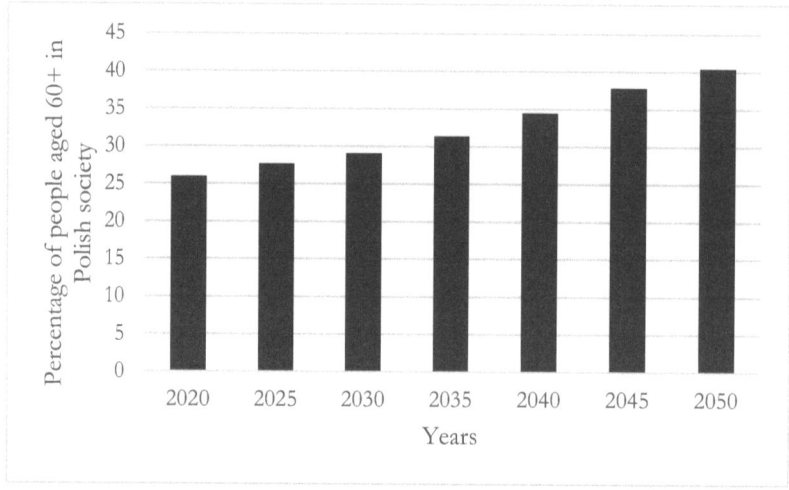

Figure 1. Percentage of people aged 60 or more in the total population. Source: Polish Central Statistical Office, 2016

A similar situation will also take place in other European countries. In view of the above-presented demographic changes, the appropriate shaping of products and services aimed at meeting the needs of an aging population, emerging from different types of aging-related dysfunctions, will take on increasing significance. Particular attention should be paid to upholstered furniture, which has direct contact with the user's body, influencing the comfort level and health of the users.

Nevertheless, the design of furniture for the elderly should focus not only on the issues related to ergonomics, but on aesthetics, quality and functionality aspects as well. The latter is understood as the adjustment of the piece of furniture to the mental and physical characteristics of the user. Thus, this is extremely important especially in the case of a user group with various types of dysfunctions. The issue of providing functional design solutions incorporated into the furniture for seniors is of paramount significance. The studies performed by Nevitt et al. (1989) show that the way of designing the home environment, including the furniture, plays a significant role in half of the identified dangerous situations that result in the fall of an elderly person. The most common factors causing dangerous situations or falls related to the interior of seniors' households include: hard-to-access light switches, e.g. in night lamps, unsteady chairs, chairs without armrests and/or with a low backrest, low chair seats, poorly adjusted functional dimensions of beds (mostly too low – which causes difficulty in getting up), and sharp furniture edges (Carter et al. 1997).

The importance of well-designed chairs was mentioned by Tinetti et al. (1994), Gill et al. (1999) and Colombo (1998). Chairs that are located near beds should provide an elderly person with facilitated transfer to the bed. This piece of furniture should also assist seniors as a support while dressing for example. The issue of the design of chairs adapted to the needs of elderly people was also raised by Šimek (2013). In his works he drew attention to the necessity to place the seat of the chair at a greater height, use armrests, ensure greater stability as well as removable, stain-resistant upholstery, mobility and the possibility to install additional elements, such as a cup holder or a small table. Studies by Fabisiak et al. (2014) confirm these results. It was found that elderly people during furniture functionality assessment paid attention to aspects such as appropriate furniture dimensions, easy-to-clean upholstery and rounded furniture edges.

One of the most important design problems is the adaptation of the functional dimensions of the furniture, especially pieces of furniture such as the bed or the armchair, to the changing anthropometric dimensions of an ageing population, as well as the needs arising from the reduced physical activity and motor skills. The ageing-related difficulties in standing up, sitting or getting out of bed are among the most frequently mentioned by elderly users of furniture. Anthropometric studies of the Polish population have shown, for example, that elderly women are shorter, heavier, have wider shoulders and a much larger torso circumference (chest, waist and hips) (Kalka 2001). Similar results, proving the smaller height and the larger circumference dimensions for elderly women, were presented by Jarosz (1998). Table 2 presents the changes in body height occurring with age.

Table 2. Changes in body height with age

Age [years]	Changes [mm]	
	Men	Women
20-35*	0	-10
35-40	0	-10
40-50	-10	-10
50-60	-10	-10
60-70	-10	-10
70-80	-10	-10
80-90	-10	-10

* average body height: men 1760 mm; women 1630 mm. Source: Bolstad et al. (2001)

Studies conducted in the Department of Furniture Design of the Poznan University of Life Sciences on a sample of 107 elderly people showed that elderly people assessing the functionality of modern upholstered furniture emphasised the lack of lumbar support for the backrests in the upholstered furniture, a frequent lack of armrests that facilitate getting up and poorly adjusted functional dimensions that are not adapted to the needs of the elderly (above all, too deep seats, too low seat height and too small seat width for armchairs). More than 50% of the surveyed people reduced the sitting discomfort by placing pillows supporting the lumbar section of the spine and reducing in this way the depth of the seat (Fabisiak et al. 2014). Another big problem is the inadequate height of the sitting or lying surface. It was noted in a series of direct interviews that elderly people or their caregivers solved this problem by placing wooden blocks, and even bricks in some cases, under the feet of the bed or the armchair. There are solutions on the market that make it possible to raise a piece of furniture by purchasing additional special feet (Figures 2 and 3), but the way they are incorporated in the piece of furniture is far from being aesthetically pleasing.

Figure 2. Furniture raiser

Source: www.disabled-world.com/

23

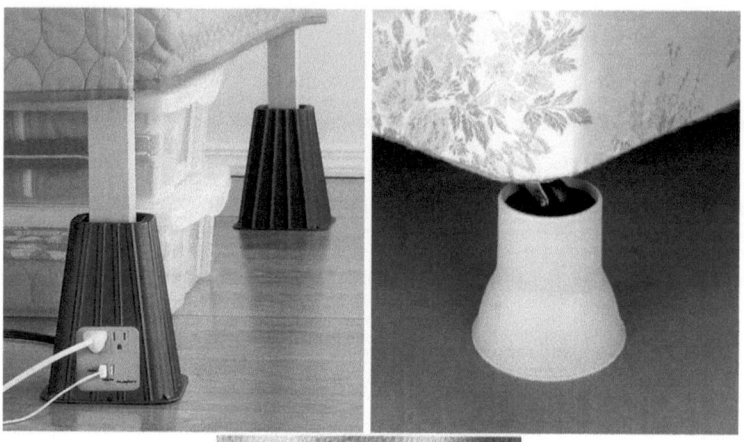

Figure 3. Examples of furniture raisers

Source: www.bedbathandbeyond.com; www.thedisabledshop.com;
www.popgiftideas.com

Another issue that should be considered when analysing the adaptation of upholstered furniture to the needs of older adults and also associated with furniture dimensions is the difficulty that seniors have in getting up and sitting down on a chair, armchair or sofa. In the upholstered furniture segment, designers noticed this issue relatively early and this has resulted in the creation of a collection of interesting solutions aimed at helping elderly people get up and sit down in an armchair. One of the most famous examples of residential furniture collections dedicated to the elderly was the collection "No Country for Old Men" shown at the Salone Internazionale del Mobile in Milan in 2012. The collection created by the design studio of Francesca Lanzavecchia and Hunn Wai includes e.g. an armchair that makes it easy to get up by stepping on the foot bar and using the weight of the user as a lever (Figure 4). It also assures stability by having armrests that follow this tilting motion (www.lanzavecchia-wai.com/projects/assunta/ 2012).

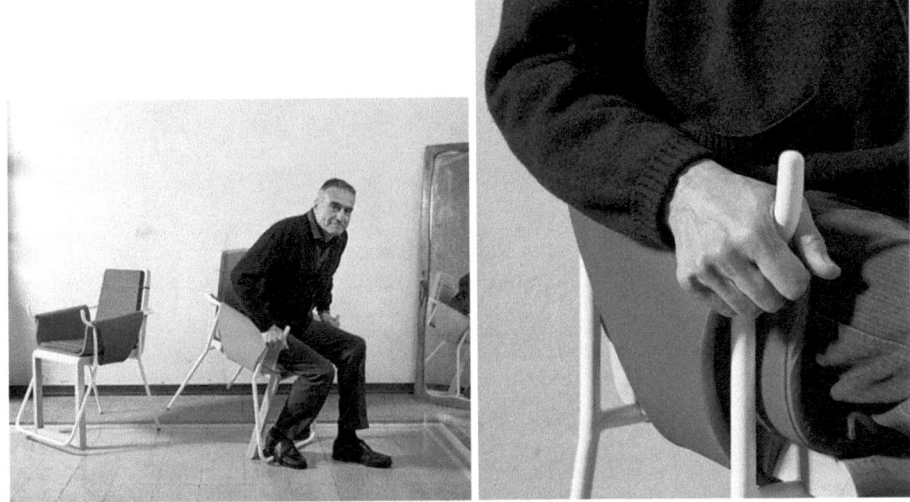

Figure 4. Assunta chair. Source: www.lanzavecchia-wai.com/projects/assunta/

On the market, there are also solutions that move the entire construction of the piece of furniture forward, supporting the elderly person in the process of getting up (Figure 5) or lifting the seat only (Figure 6).

Figure 5. Armchair supporting getting up. Source:
www.amazon.co.uk/More4Homes/

Figure 6. Armchair supporting getting up. Source:
www.savvysenior.org/article_20100920.htm

A similar solution can also be applied in chairs. The Dutch chair factory Bannink has introduced the easyUP chair (Figure 7). Thanks to a hidden torsion spring, which is charged when sitting down, the user receives a supportive boost during the process of standing up (www.markhetterich.com/projects/easyup_chair 2013).

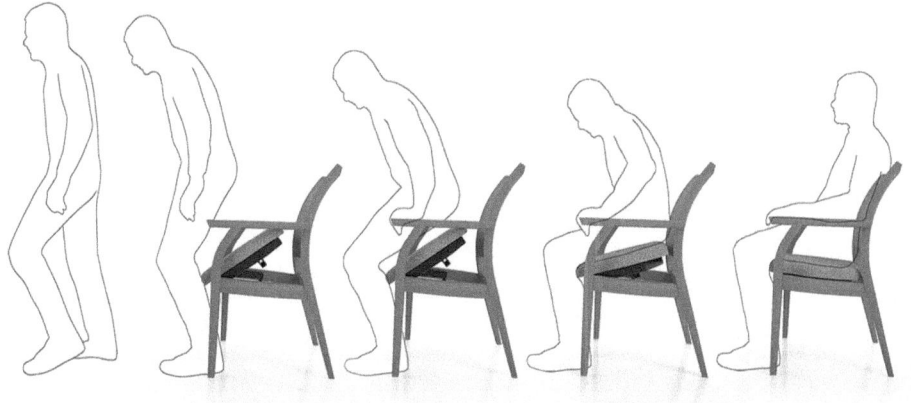

Figure 7. EasyUP chair by Bannink. Source: www.markhetterich.com/projects/easyup_chair

The British Recliner Factory, a manufacturer of reclining armchairs, also offers a product for seniors. The chair is automatically controlled and allows one to change from a completely reclining to a standing position, helping older adults to get up. Furniture settings can be freely and unrestrictedly adjusted according to seniors' needs. The chair is additionally equipped with wheels providing mobility of the piece of furniture. Moreover, it has movable armrests and an extension footrest (Figure 8).

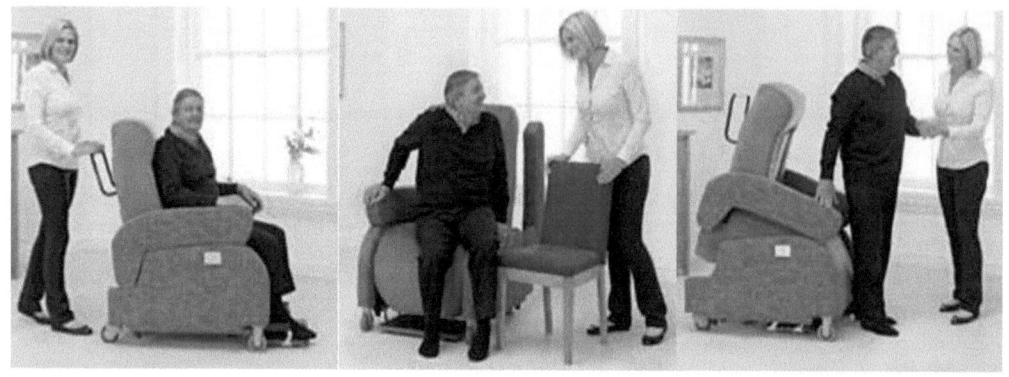

Figure 8. Riser recliner armchair by the Recliner Factory. Source:
www.reclinerfactory.com

Another British company, CareFlex, has a similar range of products in their offer.
The catalogue of products includes 8 types of furniture for seating that differ in
appearance, dimensions and some functions. All are foldable and mobile (Fig. 9).

Figure 9. Armchairs: HydroCare, HydroTilt, HydroTilt XL. Source:
www.careflex.co.uk

Another interesting example of seating furniture adapted to the needs of seniors is
reclining armchairs manufactured by the Norwegian company Helland. The product is
available in three variants, differing in additional functions. The interesting
construction of the armrest support is worth noting (Fig. 10).

28

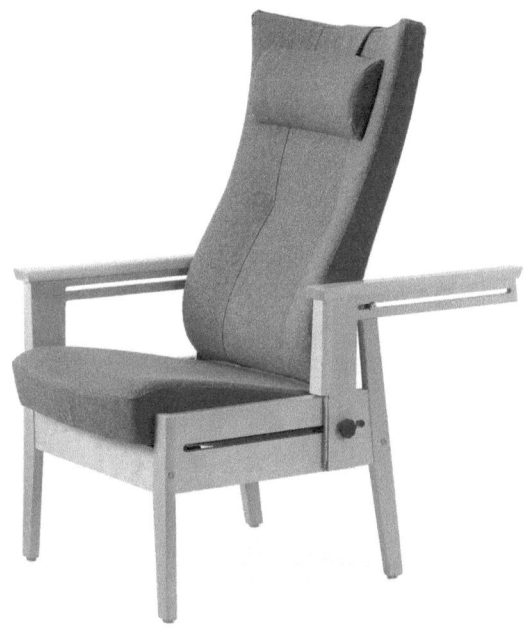

Figure 10. Bo recliner chair designed by Arild Swein Alnes and Helge Teraldsen

Source: www.architonic.com

Another Norwegian company, Kontor & Interiør, in its furniture offer has reclining armchairs for healthcare (Fig. 11) and chairs with raised seat and armrests (Fig. 12).

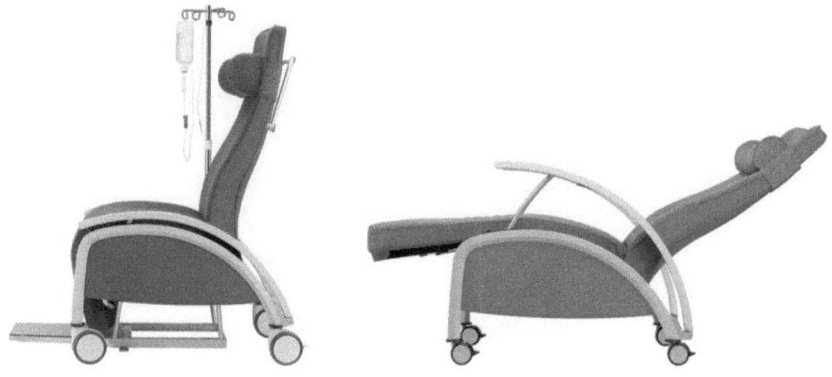

Figure 11. Reclining armchair Torras. Source: www.kinterior.no

Figure 12. Buena Nova chair. Source: kinterior.no

Also noteworthy is a series of specialised chairs – patient chairs – designed by the company Herman Miller (Figure 13). On the basis of multidisciplinary studies, it has been shown that in many cases, the sitting position taken by the patient (who had been lying for a long time) accelerated their return to health by affecting aspects such as heart rate, blood pressure and oxygen consumption, which were higher in the sitting position than in various lying positions (Herman Miller Healthcare Report 2009).

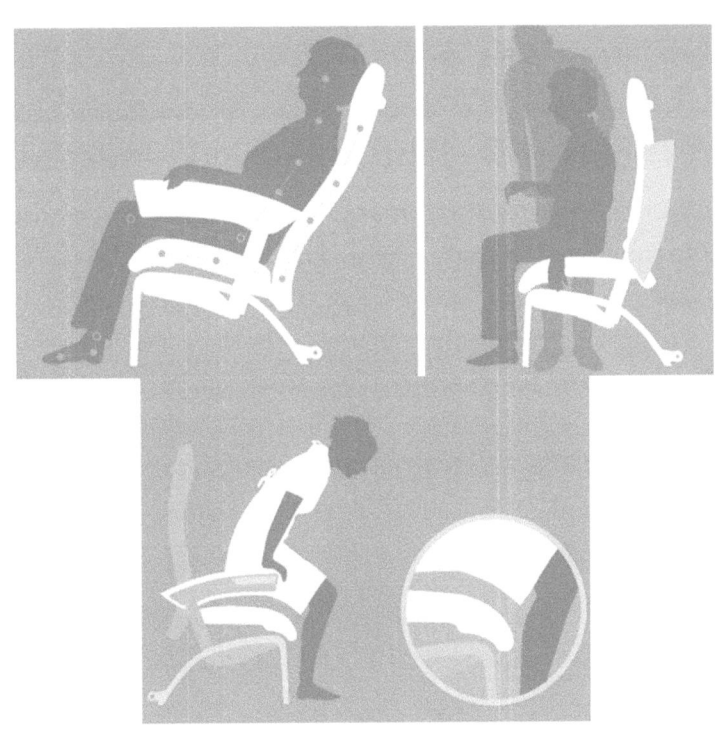

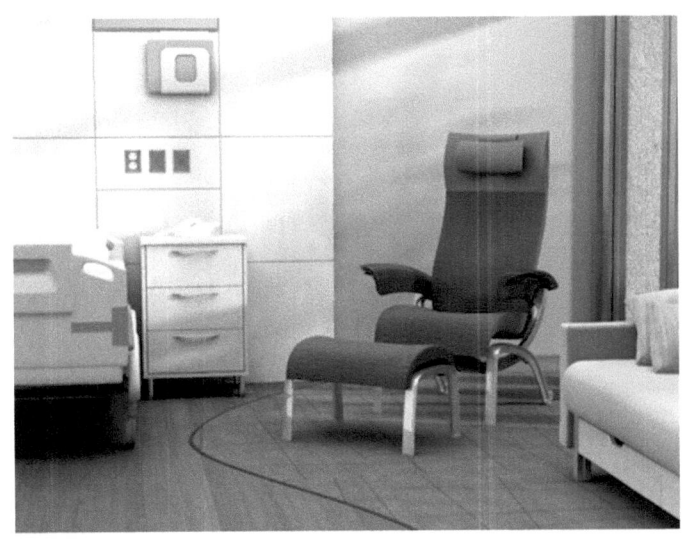

Figure 13. Nala Patient Chair by Herman Miller

Source: www.hermanmiller.com.au/products/clinical/patient-seating/nala-patient-chair.html

The Danish chair design i-SIT (Figure 14) is a perfect example of the design process involving different groups of users – the young, the elderly and those with reduced mobility – aimed at creating furniture that meets universal design principles: a philosophy of designing products that can be used by all people, to the greatest extent possible, without the need for adaptation or special design. Starting from the needs of special groups of users (having problems with back pain, arthritis, weak wrists, etc.), a model strongly rooted in Scandinavian design tradition was developed which – being adapted to the needs of more demanding users – makes sitting more comfortable even for people without any disabilities.

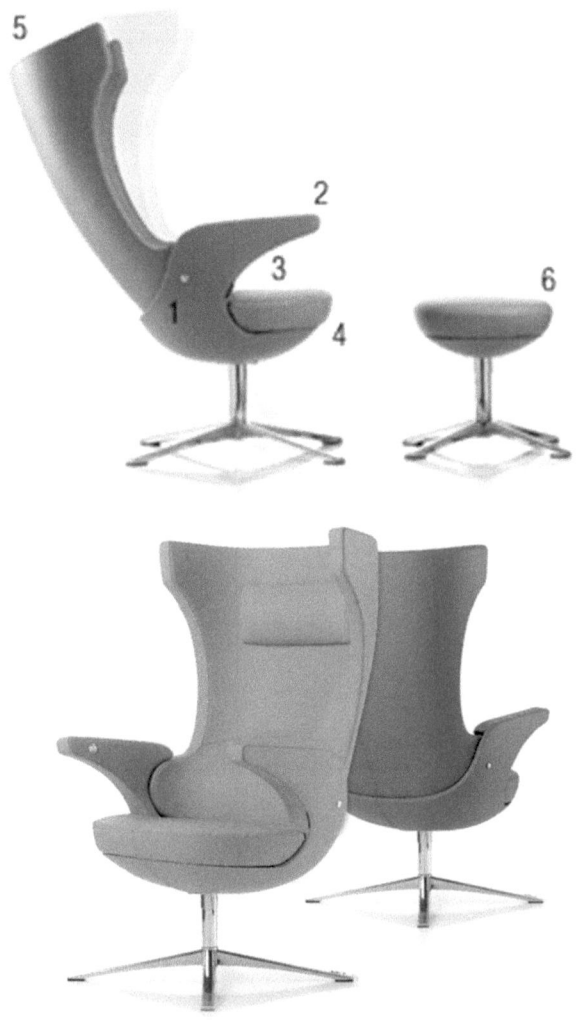

Figure 14. i-SIT. Source: www.i-sit.dk

Another crucial and functional issue is ensuring the ease of keeping the furniture clean. The armchair SOLACIA designed by Lone Storgaard and manufactured by the Danish furniture manufacturer Magnus Olesen A/S is an interesting example of combining aesthetics and functionality (Fig. 15). It has a clear and austere design, with comfortably slightly rounded shapes both in the upholstery and in the wooden armrests to provide the senior comfort while using it for many hours a day. Moreover, it is equipped with a tilting mechanism to regulate the back tilt and a detachable neck support. To make it easier to keep the armchair clean, a urinary cover and detachable seat cover in the seat cushions are available.

Figure 15. SOLACIA – designed by Lone Storgaard. Source: Magnus Olesen A/S

A furniture design problem that is only partially solved is enabling the elderly to rise on the bed. In this regard, there are several complementary accessories, examples of which are presented in Figure 16, but in many cases, their aesthetic value leaves a lot to be desired. From the viewpoint of functionality, however, these are solutions that are necessary and preferable. This is confirmed by the results of the studies carried out in the Department of Furniture Design at Poznan University in Poznan among a group of 55 people aged 65+. When describing their preferences for bedroom furniture, the respondents noted that the most important elements that increased the functionality of the furniture for lying were additional lighting sources, a bedding box and handles to assist getting up.

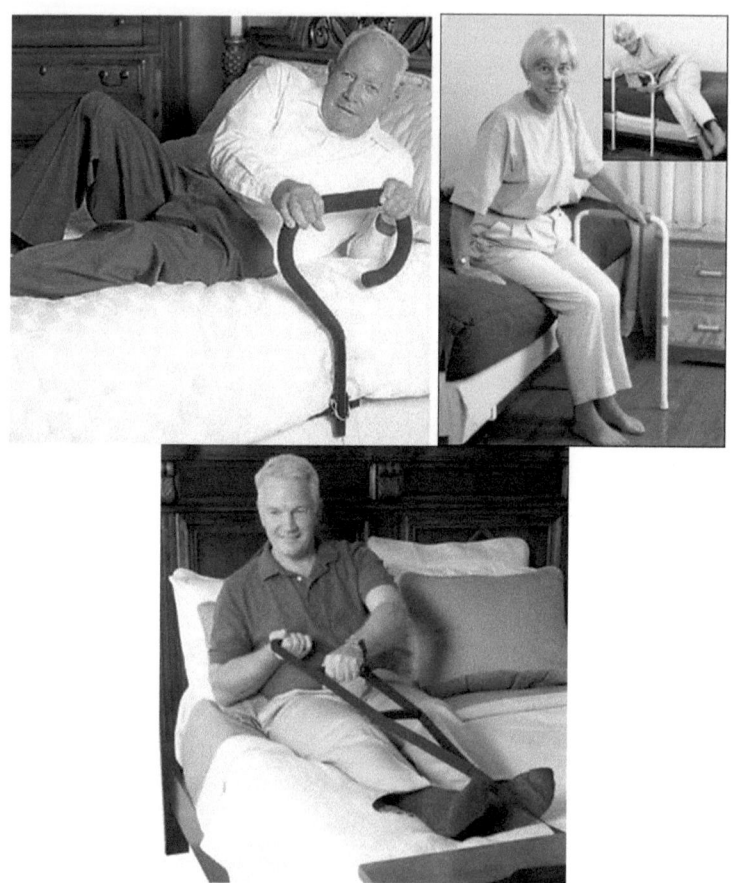

Figure 16. Bed support rail, cane and ladder. Source: www.amazon.com; www.accessibleconstruction.com/services/beds/bed-cane-bed-rail; www.agingcare.com/Products/Bedcaddie-136323.htm

Another interesting functional solution raising the comfort of seniors is a bed with an adjustable headboard offered by the Polish company New Elegance (Fig. 17).

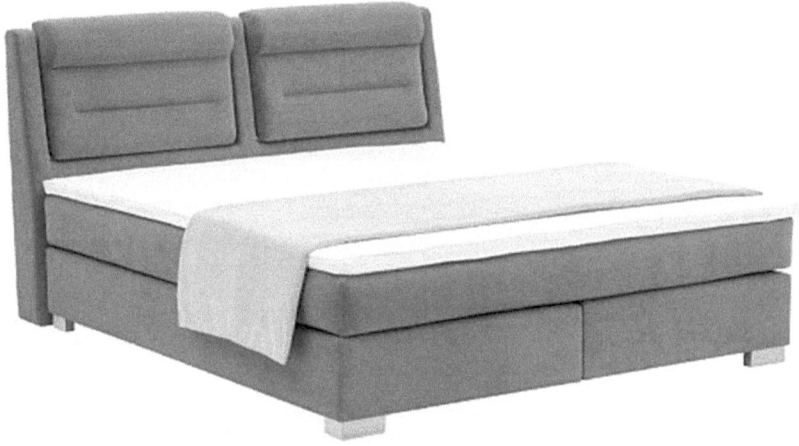

Figure 17. Bed no. 504 with adjustable headboard. Source: www.newelegance.pl

The bed offers a headboard that is adjustable at 4 levels (Fig. 18). This type of functionality is important as the bed very often is not just a sleeping zone, but also a place where we read books or watch TV. A senior, while sitting and leaning against the headboard, can adjust it to his/her preferences by modifying the angle of the headboard being at that moment the backrest. Thus, an increase of comfort of use is possible. Another interesting proposal that can be found in the presented piece of furniture is the bed base itself. It is equipped with an electrically adjustable frame, causing elevation of the back and legs (Fig. 19). This solution enables an elderly person using such a piece of furniture to easily adjust the shape of the mattress located on the frame, as a result minimizing various types of pain. In Fig. 19 the first position presents the bed in the lowered position, in the second place the headrest was raised, then the headrest together with the footrest. The last photo shows the maximum raised headrest as well as the footrest.

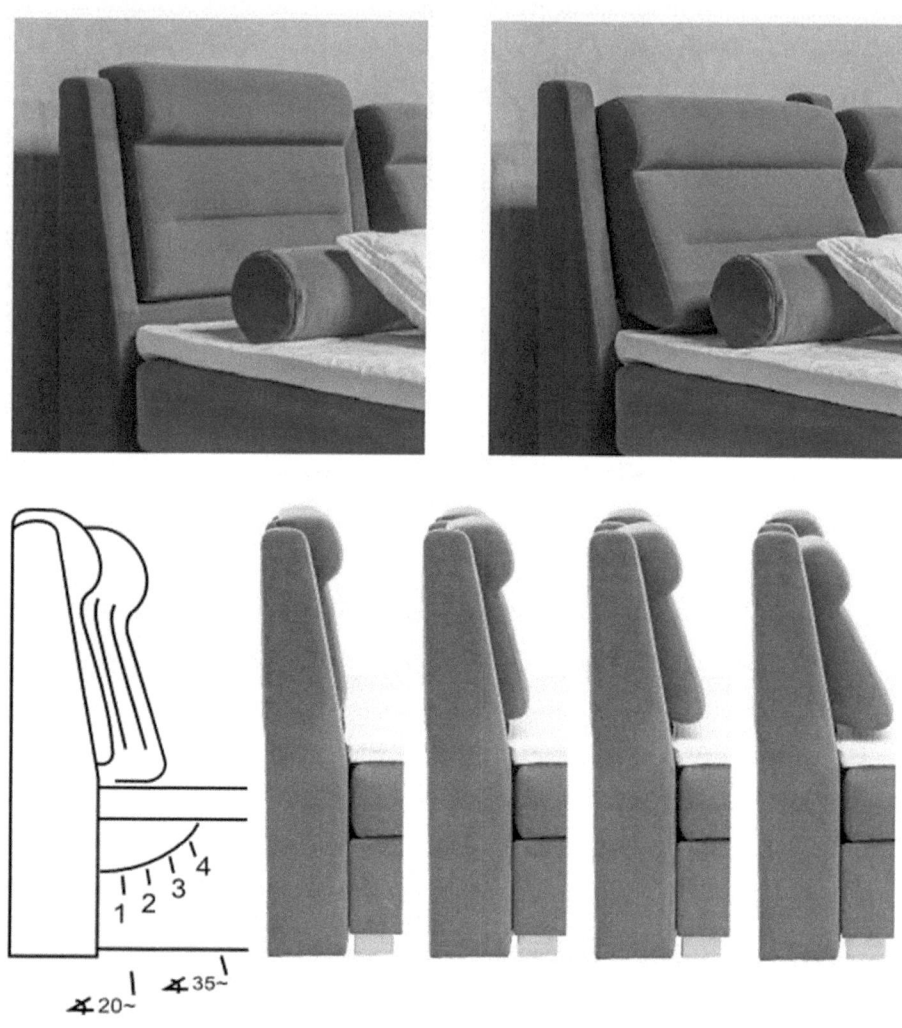

Figure 18. Bed no. 504 with adjustable headboard. Source: www.newelegance.pl

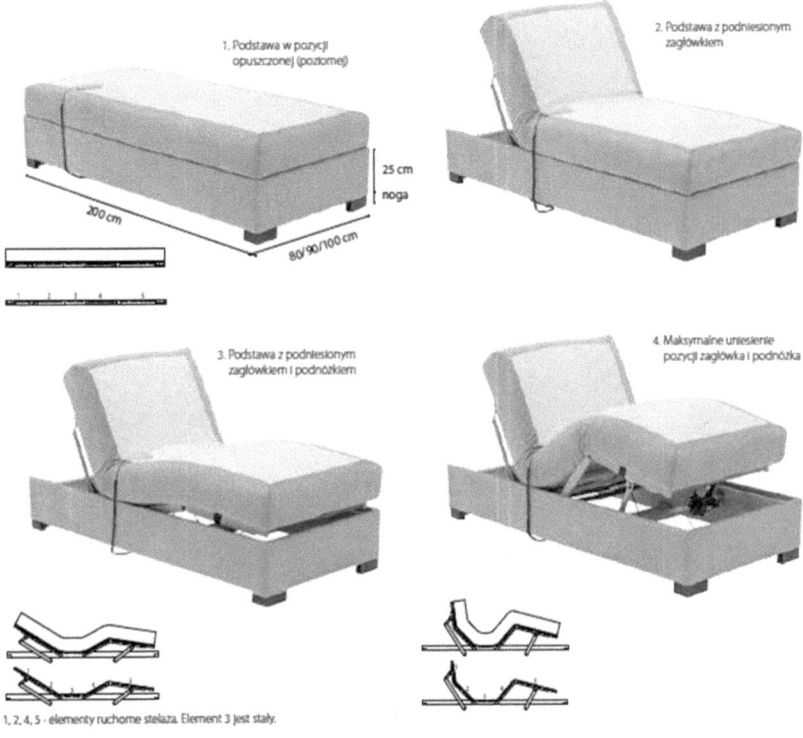

Figure 19. Bed base with electrically adjustable frame. Source: www.newelegance.pl

The lighting is an important factor in increasing not only the comfort but also the safety of using furniture. One should keep in mind that elderly people need much lighter conditions to see optimally, for example, when reading (Turner, Mainster 2008). The additional lighting integrated with the bed or an armchair was the feature most frequently indicated by seniors, who emphasised its preferred functional values. The proper lighting also helps to increase the safety of elderly people, for example, at night while getting up to go to the toilet or kitchen. Motion sensitive lighting placed under the bed, in the furniture base, may guide the senior safely across the room in the dark and reduce the risk of falling (Fig. 20).

Figure 20. Motion Active Bed Light. Source: www.amazon.com

Summary

With respect to the enormous challenges faced by furniture designers and manufacturers related to the development of a product offer tailored to the needs of the ageing population, it is very important to identify the functional requirements that make it possible to increase the comfort and safety of furniture use. Properly designed and furnished rooms in elderly people's households have a crucial influence on the quality of living and the well-being of seniors. Thus, it is essential to ensure that the furniture is comfortable and safe to use, and the main determinants should be ergonomics and functionality. It is, however, very important not to forget the aesthetic features of the products as well. One should keep in mind that well-designed products have both a high functional and design value, which in the case of furniture for the senior is still rarely observed. Fortunately, however, the increasing interest in designing for seniors recently observed is resulting in more functional and at the same time more aesthetic shaping of furniture forms for the senior population.

References

BOLSTAD, G., BENUM, B., ROKNE, A. (2001). Anthropometry of Norwegian light industry and offices workers, Applied Ergonomics 32(3): 239-246.

CARTER, S.E., CAMPBELL, E.M., SANSON-FISHER, R.W., REDMAN, S., GILLESPIE, W.J. (1997). Environmental hazards in the homes of older people, Age and Aging 26: 195 – 202.

COLOMBO, M., VITALI, S., MOLLA, G., GIOIA P., MILANI, M. (1998). The home environment modification program in the care of demented elderly: Some examples. Archives of Gerontology and Geriatrics, 26(1): 83-90.

FABISIAK, B., KŁOS, R., WIADEREK, K., SYDOR, M. (2014). Attitudes of elderly users towards design and functionality of furniture produced in Poland in the second half of the XXth century and nowadays. Ann. Warsaw Univ. Life Sci.- SGGW, For. Wood Technol. 86: 98-103.

GILL, T.M., WILLIAMS, Ch.S., ROBISON, J.T. TINETTI, M.E. (1999). A population-based study of environmental Hazards in the homes of older persons, American Journal of Public Health 89(4): 553-556.

GUS (2016): Raport Ludność w wieku 60 lat i więcej. Struktura demograficzna i zdrowie.

He, W., Goodkind, D., Kowal, P. (2016). An Aging World: 2015, U.S. Census Bureau, International Population Reports, P95/16-1, U.S. Government Publishing Office, Washington, DC.

HERMAN MILLER HEALTHCARE REPORT. (2009). Healthful Patient Seating: Perspectives from Caregivers and Researchers. Herman Miller, Inc., Zeeland, Michigan.

JAROSZ, E. (1998). Dane antropometryczne osób starszych dla potrzeb projektowania. Prace i Materiały IWP, Warszawa 1998, z. 153.

KALKA, E. (2001). Charakterystyka somatyczna kobiet starszych w wieku 60-81 lat. Dane do projektowania odzieży, VII Międzynarodowa Konferencja Naukowo-Techniczna Ergonomia Niepełnosprawnym, Łódź. Poland.

Marketing materials of Magnus Olesen A/S

NEVITT, M.C., CUMMING, S.R., KIDD, S., BLACK, D. (1989). Risk factors for recurrent nonsyncopal falls: a prospective study. Journal of the American Medical Association, 261 (18): 2663-2668.

ŠIMEK, M. (2013). Analysis of sitting furniture for elderly people. Proceedings of the XXVIth International Conference Research for Furniture Industry, Poznan, Poland.

TINIETTI, M.E., BAKER, D.I., MCAVAY, G., CLAUS, E. B., GARRETT, P., GOTTSCHALK, M., KOCH, M.L., TRAINOR, K., HORWITZ, R.I. (1994). A multifactorial intervention to reduce the risk of falling among elderly people living in the community. The New England Journal of Medicine 331 (13): 821 – 827.

TURNER, P.L., MAINSTER, M.A. (2008). Circadian photoreception: ageing and the eye's important role in systemic health. Br J Ophthalmol 92:1439–1444.

United Nations, Department of Economic and Social Affairs, Population Division (2015), World Population Prospects 2015, Data Booklet (ST/ESA/SER.A/377).

Internet Sources:

www.accessibleconstruction.com/services/beds/bed-cane-bed-rail

www.agingcare.com/Products/Bedcaddie-136323.htm

www.amazon.co.uk/More4Homes/

www.amazon.com

www.architonic.com

www.bedbathandbeyond.com

www.careflex.co.uk

www.disabled-world.com/

www.hermanmiller.com.au/products/clinical/patient-seating/nala-patient-chair.html

www.i-sit.dk

www.kinterior.no

www.lanzavecchia-wai.com/projects/assunta

www.markhetterich.com/projects/easyup_chair

www.newelegance.pl

www.popgiftideas.com

www.reclinerfactory.com

www.savvysenior.org/article_20100920.htm

www.thedisabledshop.com

Acknowledgements

This examined issues constitute a part of the project: BaltSe@nioR: Innovative solutions to support BSR enterprises in product development aimed at raising comfort and safety of seniors' home living.

This work was part-financed by the European Union (European Regional Development Fund and European Neighbourhood and Partnership Instrument).

3 | Virtual Library, an online knowledge platform about seniors – important findings

Joan Knudsen, Lifestyle & Design Cluster

When conducting international projects one of the common challenges is how to ensure that the results of the project keep generating value and change after the end of the projects. We have addressed this challenge in the Interreg BaltSe@nioR project by developing an online Virtual Library based on user needs and placed in the infrastructure of one of the partners in the project.

The purpose of this article/document is to present the motivation for making the Virtual Library, and the key findings in the development and implementation of the platform.

Purpose

The purpose of the platform was to develop an online, transnational BSR platform for knowledge sharing for furniture manufacturers, designers, students, practitioners and researchers to gain access to all relevant information from all participating countries to promote development of furniture that better meets the needs of seniors due to being based on facts and research data from the whole Baltic Sea Region (BSR).

Target groups

1. The primary target group is furniture manufacturers in the BSR, who want to better meet the needs of seniors by producing furniture that improves the quality of life of seniors and supports an autonomous life for the seniors throughout the BSR.

2. Students and designers, constructors, practitioners who want to gain knowledge about this target group and their needs and get access to tools supporting development of safe and smart furniture for seniors. Students and

45

designers who want matchmaking with companies addressing the same target group in order to develop the mentioned furniture together.

3. Technologists
4. Researchers and other relevant stakeholders such as elderly organisations who want to gain new knowledge and share knowledge about the target group of elderly people and their needs in the BSR.

Content

The content is based partly on output generated in this project and partly on existing data. We would like it to be the first place to go for information when developing furniture solutions for seniors.

Content categories have been developed based on the needs of user groups. Examples of content: ICT solutions, databases, research reports, tools and guidelines, products, methodologies, e.g. strategic design, user interaction, testing, etc.

Furthermore, users will via the Virtual Library, gain access to databases with knowledge gathered during the project.

Finally, we have integrated a match making function between designers and manufacturers and between companies via an online forum integrated into the platform. Both designers and companies can ask an open question in the forum, and then other designers, companies, researchers or students can answer this question, and users can contact each other for possible collaboration.

Functionality

User interface (UI) is in English but content varies – some content is in English, some in local languages. The user interface is flexible, allowing users to have customized entry to the platform: e.g. specific information can be sought via the country category, the topic or the search function. Searching for information can be done in two ways, either by typing search words in the free text area, or by selecting filters via the drop-down categories.

Additionally, as mentioned, the platform has an integrated forum for direct contact between users. It is also possible to contact individual users directly via the platform (not visible for the rest of the Virtual Library users). Searching for profiles is also an integrated part of the Virtual Library, as it is possible to search only for users.

Access

All content can be downloaded. Via workshops and events, we have shown target groups on how to use the Virtual Library and presented the content of the platform.

Easy platform access has been paramount in the development.

Description of development process

Identification of needs

In order to develop a long lasting and user-friendly virtual library, we started out by identifying and mapping the different user needs by sending out questionnaires to representatives from the target groups from the different BSR countries:

1. Furniture manufacturers

2. Researchers

3. Students

4. Designers and practitioners

5. Project partners

In order to get a broad variety of responses, all partners in the project were involved in sending out the questionnaires. It was important for us that the responses reflected different countries and different cultures regarding needs related to content, willingness to share knowledge, view on intellectual property rights, possible language barriers, etc.

We decided to send out separate questionnaires for project partners, so we could separate them out when identifying user needs. Before sending out the questionnaire, we also decided that the responses from furniture manufacturers would be prioritized since the whole project's goal is to support furniture manufacturers in developing products that better meet the needs of seniors.

From user groups 1-4 we received 60 responses distributed among 7 different countries and well distributed across the 4 target groups.

From there we gathered field notes and conducted a pattern recognition session in order to identify the most important and common needs within structure and functionality of the Virtual Library platform: what kind of information they need (for later categorization of knowledge), how they want to use the platform, how often, in which formats (reports, short films, pictograms, text, PowerPoint, etc.) Do they want the information? Prioritization of information, etc.

From identification of needs to blueprint

The identification of needs, field notes and pattern recognition session were highly valuable in the process of defining and describing the system requirements and use cases for the development and structure of the Virtual Library.

It also helped us in the prioritization of content and in the task of keeping complexity of use as low as possible. It formed the basis for the blueprint of the Virtual Library Architecture.

Development of the Virtual Library

The first thing after the blueprint was to develop and approve the overall design based on the rules for communication set by the project manual.

Once that was done and before actually coding the Virtual Library Platform, we (together with our sub-supplier) developed a sitemap for the whole platform (based on the use case descriptions). For each page of the Virtually Library we generated an A4 dummy layout of what kind of information and functionalities should be on which pages on the platform.

User journey test

At this point, we t*ested different user journeys to* ensure that the structure was logical and easy to use for different purposes related to the different target groups' needs. Then we began building the platform, testing with selected user representatives from different target groups to gain as much and diverse insight and feedback as soon as possible.

Identification of existing content

Collected data and content. In this phase we created an overview of available content, categories, contacts and detailed information about size, summary, language etc. for each data file and from all partners.

The developed tools are added to the Virtual Library, when they are developed. Every project partner is responsible for ensuring acceptance from the IPR holder to upload content to the Virtual Library platform.

Platform building

Development Centre UMT made a plan (together with the sub-supplier), containing an overview of all the content on each webpage in the Virtual Library. The plan was made to get a blueprint of the architecture of the platform and a user-friendly interface.

During the platform development phase, we held weekly sprint sessions and a stop-go approval phase with the sub-supplier regarding the design and functionality of the Virtual Library to ensure quality and progress.

Content building

All partners are involved in collecting and uploading content to the platform. Furthermore, they are involved in recruiting new users to the platform and disseminating information about the Virtual Library to all relevant stakeholders.

Second test phase

Students, companies and partners had the opportunity to participate in a second user journey test when the platform was in beta, during the Innovation Camp (July 2018) to ensure that all functionalities were intuitive and working correctly.

User friendly interface

The plan for the building process was made to ensure the convenience for the users, as we strive for a very user-friendly platform. The goal was to develop a platform where a manual is not needed. Instead we will develop an online guide and a FAQ page, which will be updated continuously.

Promotion of Virtual Library

The final phase concerns the promotion of the Virtual Library, because it is paramount to generate knowledge about and traffic on the platform in order to keep it alive and make sure information is disseminated in the best possible way.

We want to increase knowledge about seniors and about the potential for furniture manufacturing companies in meeting seniors' needs, preferences and gain insights to problems they face while using furniture, as well as concerning furniture characteristics such as safety, reliability, construction, etc. We will increase the BSR companies' ability to produce better products by providing them access to new knowledge. Tools, knowledge, etc., will be available for all companies interested after registering in the Virtual Library, where all knowledge databases, software, applications, presentations, publications, etc., will be accessible.

The Virtual Library has been promoted by all partners in their respective countries. It has specifically been promoted at a test workshop in Pori, Finland for furniture companies and an Innovation Camp in Herning, Denmark for students, companies, journalists, teachers and project managers. Furthermore, we promoted the Virtual Library at Stockholm Furniture Fair to a huge, diverse audience.

Important findings

When looking back on the process, one of the very important findings we have made relates to the preliminary questionnaires sent out to all user groups in all countries to identify needs and demands regarding content, functionality, IPR, language and general use of the platform prior to description of the development task. The replies created the base for the use cases for the platform and made it possible for us to make very specific technical specifications and use cases. Another positive factor concerning specifications was the involvement of an IT platform expert to assess the material we were to send out in public procurement to ensure high quality in specifications and value for money.

On the other hand, one of the main challenges has been the time span between the recruiting and having enough relevant users and content to recruit from. In spite of an effective communication strategy, we have learned that it takes time to get enough users on the platform.

A positive side-effect of choosing the sub-supplier we did was the close collaboration and possibility of physical meetings when necessary. Finally, we have strong indications that there is a need for such a platform with dedicated, specific knowledge collected in one place.

4 | Baltic Sea Region furniture SMEs today and tomorrow – survey results

Elina Priedulena, Hanse Parlament

Introduction

"It is estimated that by 2060 at least one in three Europeans will be over 65. If we take the right measures, the economy can grow; Europe boasts an innovative ICT industry with both large companies and innovative SMEs, developing many new products and services" – according to the Directorate-General for Communications Networks, Content and Technology as the responsible Commission department to develop a digital single market to generate smart, sustainable and inclusive growth in Europe. And indeed, "the silver economy has caught the attention of policy makers and economic operators alike: the ageing population promises more economic growth and jobs" (ibid.).

Experts[1] speak, however, of several "sticking points, which act as a brake on market-led developments" naming as one of most important the "information failure whereby industrial actors and service providers have been slow to recognise the impact of changing demographics and shifting consumer needs on their market" (DG Communication Networks 2018). They also state that "many innovative solutions introduced in the market are not progressing further from niche products as a result of market uncertainties, pricing issues and established business models. In many cases markets are only just developing or do not work efficiently enough" (ibid.).

In 2015 the BaltSe@nioR project took relevant action by activating and connecting leading BSR actors from the field of furniture, design, technology, ICT and robotics, economy and social sciences at national, regional and international levels to raise

---

[1] Experts involved in the European Commission study "The silver economy"

seniors' comfort and safety and at the same time enhance the capacity of innovation of the BSR furniture industry.

Aim of the survey

The Hanse Parlament together with partners conducted the online survey as part of the INTERREG BSR 2014–2020 project BaltSe@nioR to gain new insights on small and medium sized enterprises from the furniture industry in the Baltic Sea Region to their economic activities related to manufacturing, trade and services relevant for the elderly population. The main objective was to feed the project development work with the survey's findings.

The online survey was open from April 2018 to March 2019.

Methodology

The applied online survey is a web-based survey method in quantitative empirical research where the data is systematically collected, the questionnaire in the web browser being completed by the target groups. This method is widely used due to the ease of gathering data, independent of place and region, that increases the response rates as well as wide coverage of the responses by the target groups. It also makes anonymous participation possible, which statistically increases the reliability of the answers. However, one of the biggest disadvantages of the online surveys is the small influence on the distribution of the sample, which leads, as in our case, to proportionally different participation of the SMEs from the BSR countries.

Description of the applied survey tool

Online surveys are usually carried out as standardised questionnaires containing questions in a fixed order. All participants are asked exactly the same questions in an identical format and the answers are recorded uniformly. Besides anonymity in the survey, standardisation is another criterion to obtain more reliable responses. In addition, standardized questionnaires are often used because the results are easy to evaluate, compare and recognise correlations.

The used questionnaire contained semi-structured questions, a collection of closed-ended and open-ended questions that differ in the extent of predefined answer categories from which respondents can select the most appropriate one for them or multiple answers. The present questionnaire contained mostly partially standardised questions with the possibility of answering them freely via the category "other".

The questionnaire included altogether 18 questions of diverse types that determined the possible responses:

- *fact-based questions* asking for objective information and facts, for example, location of the SME. The predefined responses contained a list of countries or any other fact-based information suitable to the question.

- *questions on opinion or attitude*, for example, "How important do you think the price of the furniture is for the elderly?" The predefined responses were designed according to the five-level Likert scale, where the respondent was asked to provide the answer between 1, "not important at all", and 5, "very important".

- *action questions,* for example, "What kind of furniture are you focused on?" With predefined responses suitable to the question: kitchen, dining room, bedroom, etc.

- *appraisal questions,* for example, "What kind of products do you believe could be interesting for the elderly?" With predefined responses suitable to the question: chest, tables, armchairs, etc. (cf. Lang n. d.)

Especially in standardized surveys it is important that all respondents understand the questions both semantically (what is it about?) and pragmatically (what is meant?). The questionnaire developers paid special attention to this.

Invitation of the target group

The project partnership is designed by 11 partners from 9 Baltic Sea Region countries: Poland (PL)[2], Denmark (DK), Latvia (LV), Finland (FI), Lithuania (LT), Estonia (EE), Norway (NO), Germany (DE) and Sweden (SE) and an associated partner from Germany.

All partners were involved in attracting respondents for the survey. Each addressed the target group in the respective country by targeted writing via e-mail to the furniture associations, SMEs, etc.; placing the information on the websites and social media; putting the survey link in publications; informing the target group during workshops, conferences, fairs and other events in person.

Due to the sample of participating SMEs (n=109) from the furniture sector in the Baltic Sea Region, the findings are not representative for all SMEs of the sector located in this region. Nevertheless, the results provide the first relevant findings and sketch the trends on the SMEs' activities.

Main findings of the survey

Profile of companies in the survey

The survey includes responses by 109 businesses from 10 countries – DK, Fi, EE, LV, DE, LT, NO, PL, SE, including Russia (RU) and Belarus (BY). The participation of the companies from the latter two countries can be explained by the fact that the partner networks extend not only within the EU but also to the bordering neighbouring countries.

SMEs from Poland and Germany are most represented – every fifth company – followed by companies from Latvia as the third most frequent representatives of the

---

[2] Country codes according to ISO, International Organization for Standardization.

SME sector in the survey. The lowest number of respondents came from Norway, Belarus, Finland and Estonia.

Knowing that according to EU-wide statistical data (EUROSTAT) microenterprises[3] with fewer than 10 employees are most strongly represented in the Baltic Sea Region, it is not surprising that this size of SMEs (64%) is also most widely represented in the survey. Just under a third of those involved (28%) were small businesses with fewer than 50 employees and 8% medium sized companies with up to 250 employees.

General activities of SMEs in furniture industry

The survey started with questions about general economic activities in the furniture industry, without a focus on furniture for the elderly.

The results show that most SMEs (63%) focus on furniture for the living room, be it sofas, armchairs, side tables, shelving, etc. Almost the same proportion of companies – 47.5% and 49.5% – focus on furniture for the dining room and the bedroom. It is interesting that these three areas are named so far ahead of others – only 21% focus on office, 19% on kitchen, and 12% on bathroom furniture. The question allowed multiple choices from companies that for technical reasons could not be evaluated in this respect, so that the question remains unanswered as to whether the companies are focusing on furniture from different living and working areas at the same time or whether they are specialising in furniture from a particular living or working area. Experience with companies suggests that SMEs tend to diversify in order to be economically viable. However, this remains a hypothesis.

When asked about the materials for furniture used, the participating companies indicated a diversity of materials. At the top of the list is wood use with 86%, metal 55%, stone 28%, textiles 37% and plastic 18%. Again, several answers were possible to

---

[3] Classification of SMEs according to European Commission identified categories http://ec.europa.eu/growth/smes/business-friendly-environment/sme-definition_en (accessed 06.03.2019).

the survey participants. Based on this it can therefore be assumed that companies, by using different materials for furniture, tend to produce whole pieces of furniture rather than individual parts for completion of a piece of furniture outside the company or in cooperation with other companies.

The following table shows the distribution of responses to the question "Are you only manufacturing your products or also selling to end-users?" (n=105, 4 skipped, 1 "other" choice without no specification). Only 3 participating companies sell furniture but do not manufacture it, nearly 42% are only manufacturing and 57% of companies are integrating both manufacturing and selling in their business activity.

ANSWER CHOICES	RESPONSES	
No, we only manufacture (and sell only via business partners/dealers)	41.90%	44
Yes, we manufacture and sell directly (showroom near factory, via internet etc.)	25.71%	27
Both, we produce, sell directly and via distributors, dealers, internet etc.	31.43%	33
No own production, we just sell furniture	2.86%	3
Other (please specify)	0.95%	1

Total Respondents: 105

Consequently, two questions arose: firstly, "who are the customers of the furniture products?" The answers show that private households with almost 91% account for the largest share of customers of furniture products. The second largest share of 40% are private companies and the third largest one are players from the public sector. Secondly, "how are the new products designed?" In most cases the design process takes place in the same company. However, a small portion has outsourced the design process and every fourth company has stated that it designs furniture based on customer wishes.

And finally, given that ICT use and the digitization process and progress in companies have been topical for a while now, it was natural to find out to what extent companies from the furniture industry integrate ICT solutions in furniture (keyword *smart home*). The result is pretty sobering: only 13% of companies in the survey integrate

ICT in the furniture. Accordingly, 87% do not do it yet. So far, ICT-based furniture has been designed and manufactured in DK, DE, NO, SE and PL.

Activities of companies in the furniture sector for the elderly

One of the key questions in the survey was "Do you already create furniture specifically for the elderly (60 years and over)?" The graph reveals the distribution of answers: nearly 27% already create furniture for the elderly and a good two thirds of the companies involved in the survey do not do so. It is positive, however, that 33.33% of those can imagine creating furniture for the elderly in the future.

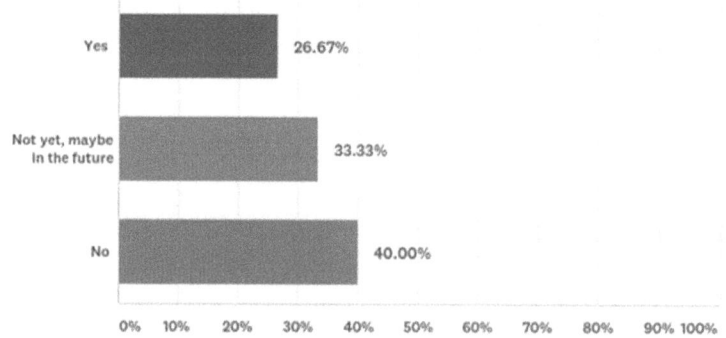

It is worth breaking down the given answers according to the geographical location of the enterprises (see the chart below): significantly more companies that have already been creating furniture for the elderly came from western Baltic Sea Region countries: DK, SE, NO and DE. LV, LT, PL, RU, BY are on the other hand the countries that clearly predominate in the answers with "No, I do not create furniture for the elderly yet", and companies from almost all countries can imagine focussing on furniture for the elderly in the future.

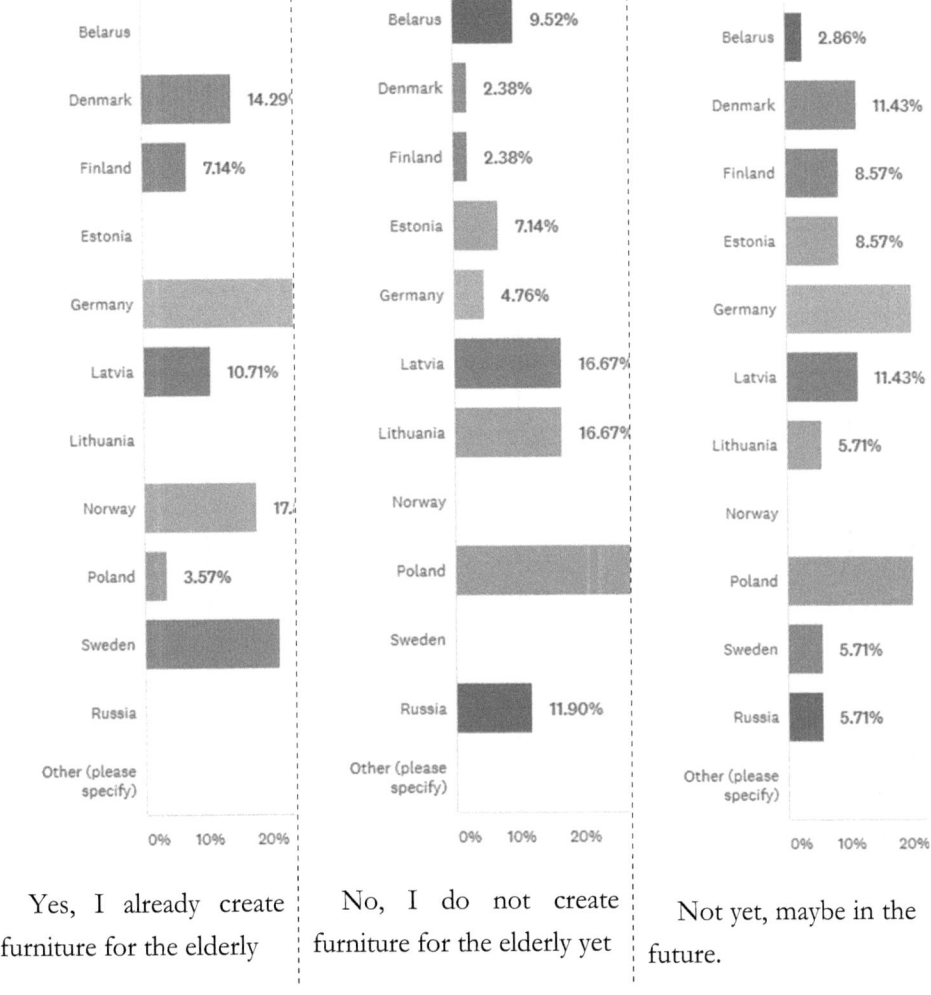

Yes, I already create furniture for the elderly	No, I do not create furniture for the elderly yet	Not yet, maybe in the future.

The next question was directly related to the previous one "Why do the companies not create furniture for the elderly?"

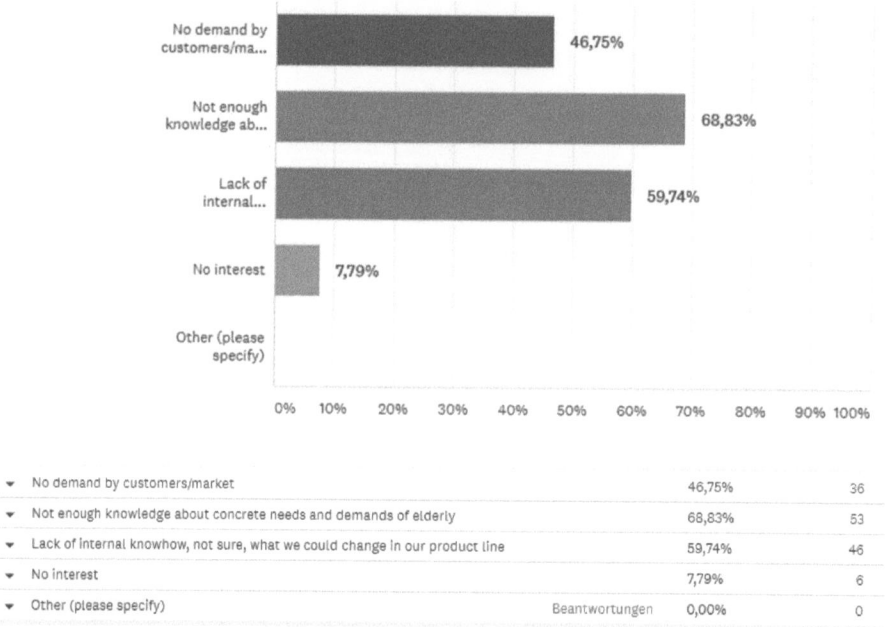

▼ No demand by customers/market	46,75%	36
▼ Not enough knowledge about concrete needs and demands of elderly	68,83%	53
▼ Lack of internal knowhow, not sure, what we could change in our product line	59,74%	46
▼ No interest	7,79%	6
▼ Other (please specify)	Beantwortungen 0,00%	0

The most frequently chosen reason in nearly 70% of cases was the lack of knowledge about the specific needs and demands of the elderly. This would support the sticking point identified by the Directorate-General in the introduction about the information failure that prevents the industrial actors and service providers from recognising the impact of changing demographics and shifting consumer needs on the market (DG for Communication Networks 2018).

Looking at the frequency of responses to this question, an interesting fact comes to light. This is the only question skipped by so many respondents – a total of 32. All other questions were skipped by an absolute maximum of 4 participants. One assumption could be that the companies have simply not yet addressed the issue, so they had no concrete answer to the question and preferred to skip it.

Since certain differences are noticeable in the behaviour of companies by region – east and west of the Baltic Sea – throughout the survey, the responses to this question were also examined according to this aspect.

Responses by companies from the eastern part of the Baltic Sea - BY, EE, LV, LT, RU.

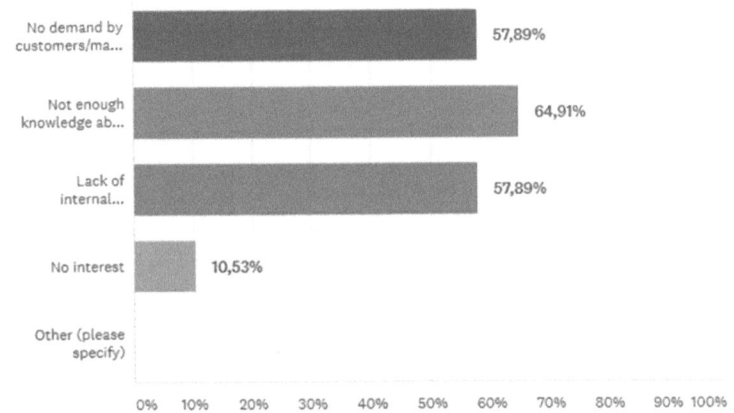

Answered: 57   Skipped: 4

Responses by companies from the western part of the Baltic Sea – DK, DE, FI, SE, NO.

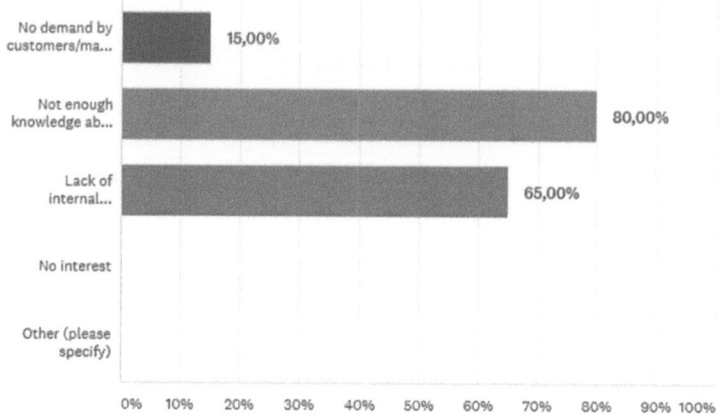

When comparing the answers between the regions, two differences are noticeable: significantly more companies from eastern BSR countries believe that there is no demand on the market for age-appropriate furniture among older people and some companies, albeit a small proportion of them, of the same countries admitted that they simply have no interest in furniture manufacturing for this population group. In the western countries, however, not a single company decided on this answer.

When asked about furniture products that would be most interesting for the elderly, the greatest consensus was found in kitchen and bathroom furniture, in the bedroom the bed, and in the living area the armchair. However, would there also be buyers among the older ones? The next question – "How important do you think the price of the furniture is for elderly?" – should give a hint on this.

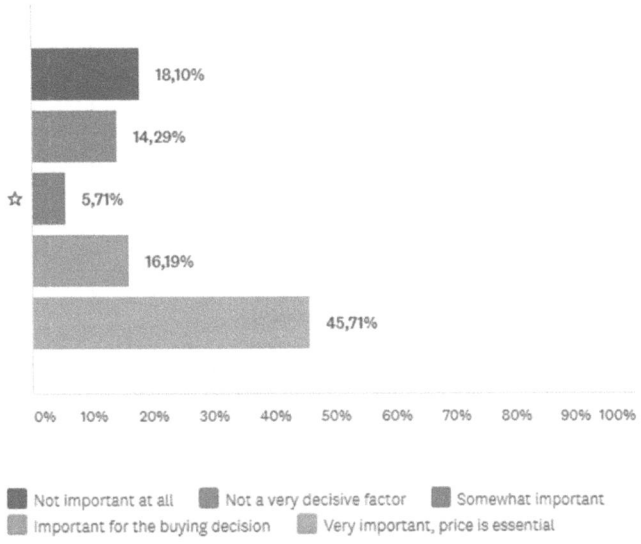

The participating companies from eastern and western parts of the BSR assessed the price issue completely differently. While in companies from BY, EE, LV, LT and RU 67% said the price is essential, in the DK, DE, FI, SE, and NO only 16% shared the same opinion. Accordingly, in western BSR countries 43% of SMEs believe that the price is not important at all.

Regarding the question about the importance of comfort of furniture, companies from eastern BSR countries think that comfort is

- not important at all – 22%,

- not a very decisive factor – 39%

- very important – 22%

In contrast, companies from western BSR countries are of the opinion that comfort is

- not important at all – 9%

- not a very decisive factor – 16%

- very important – 44%

It also seems that there are region-specific differences in opinion by companies in durability and functionality of furniture for the elderly:

Durability	Total %	West %	East %
Not important at all	23	21	25
Not decisive, durability hardly matters	27	28	43
Somewhat important, should last a bit	28	42	18
Important for the buying decision	11	9	12
Very important, durability is essential	2	0	3

Functionality	Total %	West %	East %
Not important at all	13	5	18
Not decisive, durability hardly matters	28	28	28
Somewhat important, should last a bit	25	19	29
Important for the buying decision	23	30	18
Very important, durability is essential	12	19	7

In the last question, the companies were asked for their opinion on "how important do you believe it is to take time to consult the elderly and ask for their specific needs", when creating furniture for them?

Consultation and specific needs	Total %	West %	East %
Most important, they need a lot of information	25	53	18

Important, they need more advice than other customers	14	14	28
No difference to other customers	40	26	30
Usually not important	15	7	18
Not very important at all, they know what they want	5	0	7

Based on the last responses, it can be concluded that companies from eastern countries of the Baltic Sea Region consider the price of furniture to be decisive for the buying decision, and that other furniture characteristics such as comfort, durability and functionality are subordinate to the price or even do not matter at all. This does not correspond with the view of companies from western BSR countries, where the SMEs attach little or no importance to the price and consider other furniture features such as comfort, durability and functionality to be decisive for the purchase decision, or more decisive than the price.

Regarding the question about the importance of consultation and asking about the needs of the elderly, every second company from western Baltic Sea Region countries finds the consultation and inclusion of the specific needs of the elderly most important. While not even every second company in the eastern countries considers this to be most important, 28% consider it at least important. In both groups of countries, however, almost equal groups find that there is no difference from other customers.

Conclusions

If a "typical" company from the furniture industry in the Baltic region had to be described after the evaluation, the profile would look something like this: micro-enterprises that concentrate on the production of living room furniture, so that private households are the most important end consumers. The furniture is mainly made of wood, but since they are most likely to make a whole piece of furniture, other materials are also used. The piece of furniture is designed in house and does not integrate ICT into its use. The "typical" company from the Baltic region does not yet produce furniture for older people but is open to it. However, it should be better informed about the needs and demands of the elderly.

References

Directorate-General for Communications Networks, Content and Technology, Digital Single Market, Policy, Policies for Ageing Well with Information and Communication Technologies (ICT): https://ec.europa.eu/digital-single-market/en/ageing-well; last update October 1, 2018 (Accessed 31.01.2019).

European Commission study "The silver economy" conducted by Technopolis and Oxford Economics in 2018: https://ec.europa.eu/digital-single-market/en/news/silver-economy-study-how-stimulate-economy-hundreds-millions-euros-year (Accessed 05.02.2019).

Lang, Sabine (n. d.), Empirische Forschungsmethoden: https://www.uni-trier.de/fileadmin/fb1/prof/PAD/SP2/Allgemein/Lang_Skript_komplett.pdf (Accessed 05.02.2019).

5 | The BaltSe@nioR system – addressing seniors' needs with Smart Furniture

Katharina Langosch, Jörg Güttler, Thomas Bock, Technical University Munich

Sari Merilampi, Santeri Saari, Venni Ihanakangas, Anja Poberznik, Satakunta University of Applied Sciences

Trine A. Magne, Sigrid Bye Skille, Siri Munch Wahl and J. Artur Serrano, NTNU/Norwegian University of Science and Technology

Demographic change and an ageing society are presenting the furniture industry with new challenges as well as new opportunities for opening up new markets for new target groups. An innovative response to the needs and requirements of elderly people living in dignity in their own environment can be provided by the use of intelligent information and communication technologies (ICT) integrated into the furniture. The BaltSe@nioR project focuses on developing such Smart Furniture as assistive, affordable and intelligent solutions for supporting seniors in their daily life by addressing their desire to live independently and to feel secure and safe. The integration of the ICT solutions is unobtrusive and does not give the impression of senior housing or of a person in need of constant medical attention.

In a close collaboration between the ICT partners from the Norwegian University of Science and Technology (NTNU), Satakunta University of Applied Sciences (SAMK) and the Technical University of Munich (TUM), as a collective outcome, the BaltSe@nioR System (Figure 1) was developed. It consists of different age-appropriate ICT furniture units/modules such as Fall Detection, Mobile Robot, Magic Mirror, ReAbleChair, Smart Chair, etc., which are connected to one common Modular BaltSe@nioR Server. Each of the ICT furniture units/modules addresses different needs of the elderly and can be added to or removed from the server according to the current health status or private requirements of the seniors. Thus, the modularity concept offers the opportunity to extend and adapt the system over time to the individual needs of those of advanced age, if required.

The different ICT furniture units/modules, with their specific focus on seniors' needs as well as their functionality, are presented below. Furthermore, forming the BaltSe@nioR System, the ICT modules were presented as prototypes in the MeWet home environment in Ulvila, Finland, during two weeks in November 2018 and were tested by seniors as well as other visitor groups (caretakers, students of elderly care, and people with physical and cognitive disabilities). The feedback provided during the field test is summarised as well.

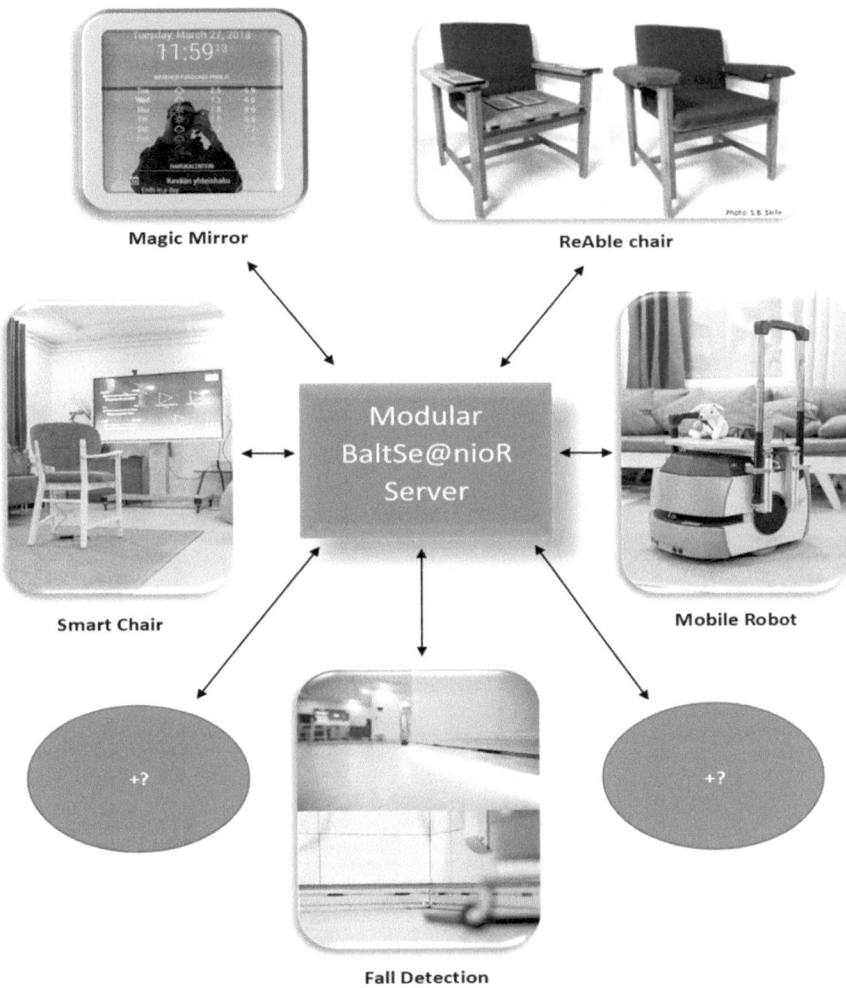

Figure 1. Visualisation of the BaltSe@nioR System

Fall Detection and Mobile Robot

Seniors' needs:

Elderly people prefer to live independently in their own environment instead of in a retirement/care home. However, with increasing age, limited mobility or impairment, the fear grows that they might slip or fall in their home and not be able to help themselves. There are various reasons why a fall may occur, e.g. dizziness, unwariness or unconsciousness, etc. In the worst case, if no help is available after a fall, the affected person may remain lying unnoticed and die as a consequence. In addition, often there is the health risk of suffering from complications due to e.g. fractures or prolonging the recovery process due to secondary diseases and then not returning to their own home afterwards.

Older individuals face such challenges of wanting to live independently on the one hand and yet are afraid of being helpless on the other. These situations cause worry and stress. Additionally, elderly persons prefer to help themselves rather than ask for help and feel uncomfortable when any assistance systems in their home are clearly visible and give the impression of a senior's/care house.

Solution to address seniors' needs:

Fall Detection (FD), in combination with the **Mobile Robot (MR)**, responds to the needs of older persons to reduce their fear and anxiety of falling and provide a feeling of security and safety in their own environment. In the case of a fall, this assistance system is able to detect the fall, send the MR to the person in need of support and give the fallen person the opportunity to either stand up self-sufficiently using the handles fixed onto the robot or to call someone, e.g. caregivers or relatives, for help.

Due to the unobtrusive integration of the FD into a baseboard (the design of the baseboard is freely selectable according to the conditions of the existing home) and the discrete implementation of the docking station of the MR in a cabinet (designed according to the existing furniture), the seniors' requests regarding not giving the impression that it is a senior housing can be met. Furthermore, the MR is equipped with a wooden plate, which serves as a table or butler for bringing/carrying goods such as medicine, a glass of water or the phone rather than as an aid.

Functionality of the solution:

Fall Detection (FD) follows the concept of an infrared light barrier system and consists mainly of two infrared emitters and several self-developed fall detection sensors. The fall detection sensors are designed to be integrated into a baseboard so that the system can be adapted to any conditions of an existing room, even a bathroom. The solution of using the baseboard for the FD offers seniors and the furniture industry possibilities for variation regarding the selection of the design of the baseboard according to the individual's preferences or existing furnishings. The only requirement for the baseboard is a notch for inserting the fall detection sensors.

The FD system, which can be embedded in different rooms of an apartment or home, is connected to the MR via a server. Since the FD is able to distinguish whether a person is standing or lying on the floor – a fallen person covers a higher number of sensors than a standing person – in case of an emergency, if a person has fallen, the FD sends the MR to the person in need. Through the implementation of speech recognition and sound output to the MR, communication between the person and the robot using the question "Do you need help" and the answers "Yes" or "No" is possible in order to assess whether help is required. If the command "Yes" is followed, the MR assists the fallen person either with the integrated handles allowing the person to get up self-sufficiently or with further devices such as a mobile phone placed on the table of the MR for calling a nurse or relatives for help. With a "No" response or if the event is finished and the FD does not recognise any emergency any more, the MR returns to its docking station hidden unobtrusively in a cabinet waiting for further instructions from the FD. The communication language can be selected according to the mother tongue of the elderly.

Feedback about the solution:

Fall Detection (FD), in combination with the **Mobile Robot (MR)**, was tested as one joint system by different stakeholders during the field tests in the MeWet home environment in Ulvila, Finland. The feedback given by the test people was in general positive. The purpose of these prototypes was found to be clear to understand and, for most of the test subjects, the prototypes were easy to use. Safety and the support offered by the system were important factors for considering both prototypes in the own home and selecting them as useful ambient assistive living (AAL) systems. The field test with the seniors also confirmed that, in case of a fall, older persons would prefer to handle the situation by themselves. This shows that the developments of the prototypes conform to the seniors' needs. However, there have also been concerns mentioned as to whether the robot would replace humans or simply offer additional assistance.

Furthermore, some weak points and potential for improvement could be identified during the tests. In particular, regarding the MR, some seniors proposed that the handles should provide assistance in lifting up the fallen person or additional legs for more stability while standing up. Moreover, the seniors suggested that it would be valuable if the MR could be additionally controlled by voice commands and for the opportunity to call for or talk to the MR. A robotic arm fixed onto the MR could be another useful feature for helping with daily activities or it could be used to carry heavy objects, e.g. shopping bags.

Magic Mirror

Seniors' needs:

Elderly people might develop problems with their memory at some point in their lives. They may have to start using different tools and methods to remember what particular tasks they have to do during the day. Daily tasks can consist of taking medication or going to a doctor's appointment, but in some cases even basic tasks such as eating can be forgotten without assisting the person's memory. The rising number of elderly people creates a market for different types of memory refreshing and assisting systems for different stages of memory problems.

Solution to address seniors' needs:

To address these types of cognitive, memory-based problems, the Magic Mirror can help elderly people with different memory impairing conditions. The Mirror works both as an information display and a regular mirror; so for example being able to check what's on the calendar while combing one's hair might be a good way of getting this type of memory refreshing information. The mirror is based on a modular platform so it can be customized to also give other information that the user might enjoy, such as news headlines and weather forecasts. The mirror also has other functionalities: it has a facial recognition system that can be used to check how often the mirror is used and other people such as relatives or caretakers can send messages to it. The facial recognition also works as a way to customize the content the mirror displays for each inhabitant.

Functionality of the solution:

The functionality of the Magic Mirror can be highly customized based on the user. It very much depends on the user what kind of modules are needed and also what the user wants to see on the screen. If the user has problems with their memory, different calendar and reminder modules are useful for helping them. If the user is susceptible to not being able to get up from bed, the facial recognition can be used to monitor the use. If the person doesn't "log in" to the mirror with their face every morning, relatives or caretakers can suspect something is wrong.

Feedback about the solution:

Feedback about the Magic Mirror has been mostly positive. Many of the interviewed persons also had ideas on what type of features they would like to see on the mirror. Some of them include video playback on the mirror, a voice+video call possibility and touch screen interactivities. One new valuable developmental idea is related to severe memory impairment: the mirror could "disappear" if a memory impaired person stood on it (as they might be afraid of the reflection).

People have also given positive feedback of the mirror frame, saying it's nice that the frame design is rather traditional, so on the surface it doesn't look like a technological gadget. Negative comments have mostly concerned the technical side of the mirror's software. For example, adding appointments to the calendar that's visible on the mirror requires the use of a digital, cloud-based calendar. Also, changing what modules are on the screen requires programming at the moment, so it has to be done by someone who has knowledge of that. Both have been seen as nuisances for the end user.

In general, people easily started thinking of ideas how to use or improve the prototype, which indicates understanding of the functionality and added value.

ReAbleChair

Seniors' needs:

With an ageing population, focus on functional decline is crucial. Changes in physical function are important to detect early and objective measurements from daily activity, for example the action of rising from a chair, can provide valuable information about older adults' functional status. Natural chair-rises including spontaneous use of the chair's armrests is therefore important to assess. Furthermore, training physical and cognitive function regularly is of importance in active aging. The ReAbleChair prototype collects high quality measurements of the sit-to-stand movements and can also be used as a tool in rehabilitation to train physical and cognitive function in association with exergames.

Solution to address seniors' needs:

The ReAbleChair prototype is a redesigned chair with integrated force plates. The force plates are hidden under the chair seat and the armrests pads, so that the chair may be used as natural furniture in the older adults' home. Using the ReAbleChair, automated and continuous assessment of physical function can therefore be done in the older adult's home environment. The information collected can be used to analyse and evaluate physical function and in clinical reasoning. In addition, the ReAbleChair prototype has the possibility to play different exergames simply by moving in the chair, using pressure on the force plates. Such exergames can provide both physical and cognitive training. The ReAbleChair provides an assistive solution for older adults living at home in the pursuit of active and safe ageing.

Functionality of the solution:

The ReAbleChair prototype was mainly developed with the intention to integrate technology in furniture used by older adults living at home, and furthermore, to give feedback on how older adults move when they stand up and sit down. This information can provide health professionals (e.g. physio- and occupational therapists) quantitative data on physical function collected in a natural environment in the older adult's home.

The chair provides information on how the older adult is seated, and if seated in an unsafe way when starting to stand, this can in the future be used to program a voice command giving instructions to correct the positioning. This is to prevent an unsafe situation when standing up and also to prevent the older adult from falling.

As mentioned above, the chair may be used to train physical function during rehabilitation. There are many options with regard to exergames that can be played using the force plates. These games can be customized with regard to the older adults' interests and skills.

Feedback about the solution:

The ReAbleChair was developed as an ICT solution to collect information on physical function and it was presented as such in the MeWet home. The chair's ability to be used as a tool to play games to exercise both physical and cognitive function was not presented or evaluated. The functionality and the purpose of the chair, as presented, were well understood. Some participants declared to be surprised by the possibility to receive feedback on physical function as they experienced it.

The idea of the chair monitoring health outcomes was commented on as useful by health professionals as well as the older adults. Others commented that it could be helpful if it could tell you if you have been sitting too long, both in a home or in a work-related environment. The question of who is in charge of the data was raised as a concern by the health professionals; however, they could see the benefit of using these data in therapy sessions when the older adult lived in remote areas.

A goal for this ICT solution was that it should be natural furniture in one's home; in that sense it was observed that nobody paid much attention to the chair before it was shown and presented as a prototype in the MeWet home. As the ReAbleChair was developed by redesigning an old chair with the intent to show the possibility to integrate ICT solutions in existing furniture in older adults' homes, comments on the design are not presented here.

Overall, the feedback on the ICT solution was positive. Both health professionals and others visiting the MeWet home understood the purpose of the chair and also could see possibilities for further developments.

Smart Chair

Seniors' needs:

Staying active is important for elderly persons in order to minimize the risk of injuries, but exercising is something that the elderly are unlikely to do. The exercise movements they have to make are very repetitive and having to exercise quickly becomes a chore. On a positive note, the elderly do not have to exercise hard; even slight training can help to stay active. Unfortunately, not all elderly people have easy access to a gym or the chance for physiotherapy.

Solution to address seniors' needs:

To get people motivated to move and do exercises, the **Smart Chair** was developed. The chair lets the elderly train without it really feeling like such. This is done through games which motivate the elderly to move every part of the body at least a little to progress in the game. It is not necessary to move much; small movements are enough for the elderly to train. Addressing the problem that people cannot always go to a place where they would exercise, the chair has been made fully wireless and light so it can be easily installed in private apartments. In addition to it being wireless and light, it also looks like an everyday chair so it can stay in the living room like a normal chair. Complementary to the chair the games have been made for Android devices, so it is possible to play them on a phone, tablet or on a bigger screen like a smart TV. The chair is connected to the device via Bluetooth. The movements of the elderly are measured through nine pressure sensors under the sitting surface and are unobtrusive so as not to stigmatize the elderly. The provided games can be adjusted to the individual needs through slow/fast and easy/hard adjustments.

Functionality of the solution:

The functionality of the solution is the ability to play games developed specifically for the smart chair. These games provide different types of physical activity and movement for the user without forgetting the entertainment side of the training. The chair games are currently sport-themed: ski jump and snowboarding. In the ski jump the game is controlled by standing up and sitting down, and the snowboarding is controlled by balancing left and right to control the snowboarder. Also included is a ball throwing game for the use of upper body muscles, which does not necessarily need the chair. All of these games track high scores, which can be used to track the progression of the player's physical ability. It also challenges the player to do better in order to beat their older score or someone else's score if the user plays the games together with their friends or relatives.

Feedback about the solution:

Feedback on the solution has been very positive. People liked the chair's design, the games and how they worked together as a way of physical activity. Many people wanted to try the games again after playing it once, likely to improve their score. The negative feedback was mostly targeted at the display we used for the games. It was an ~60-inch tablet, which is not a device everyone owns. The main idea with the tablet was that we could use it for the ball throwing game because it had a touchscreen. Also, one of the important aspects of it was the full Android system it was equipped with, so it was easy to develop the games using a smaller tablet or a phone with an Android operating system. However, the most likely device people would use the chair with is a flat screen TV without a touchscreen, so some modifications to the game would be necessary.

The games themselves were relatively well understood and seniors were relatively willing to try the games. Those not willing to play themselves were still very interested in watching others play. The gaming increased social interaction (people cheering, giving advice, talking about the winter Olympics…) and was described as a good means to activate people to take more exercise. Multiplayer games were mentioned to potentially lower the threshold to play and further increase the social effect of the games. Various ideas were mentioned about which situations the games could be played in, including group homes and waiting lobbies. It was also mentioned that the data the games and the chair sensors produce might also be used for evaluating changes in ability to function.

3D-printed furniture handles

As an addition to the ICT solutions, several furniture handles were designed and printed using 3D technology. Some of the physical changes that occur in aging are weakened hand grip, degenerative changes in fingers and hands, and therefore painful grip due to e.g. rheumatoid arthritis. Often existing handles do not provide a good grip or the space between the handle and the cabinet or drawer is too small and thus difficult to fit the hand in. 3D printing enables a fully customizable design of handles, which results in more functional use.

Conclusion of the test feedback

Generally, the prototypes were well accepted, and no general negative attitude was noticed. The feedback indicated the presented prototypes to be meaningful and solving real problems. Some concerns mentioned were related to the visual appearance, the potential costs and the fact the prototypes are not yet commercially available. The testing as such provided an enjoyable moment, where the participants felt like being part of technological development (free comments from seniors). People were eager to comment and suggest improvements to the prototypes. One valuable learning outcome which was further clarified was the essential role of branding. The seniors of today do not want to be categorized as "seniors needing help". This is also why the marketing should be done accordingly, offering customizable solutions for anybody instead of emphasizing seniors as a target group: "customizable (even luxurious) products especially made for your needs".

6 | Creative design workshops with students

Vineta Kreigere, Barbara Ābele, Art Academy Latvia
Ruth-Helene Melioranski, Estonian Academy of Arts
Beata Fabisiak, Robert Kłos, Poznan University of Life Sciences
Joan Knudsen, Lifestyle & Design Cluster

Creative design workshops with students

Within the framework of the BaltSe@nioR project three universities collaborated in the organization of creative design workshops with students: the Art Academy of Latvia, the Poznan University of Life Sciences and the Tallinn University of Technology. The objective was to support enterprises based in the Baltic Sea Region in product development aimed at adapting products to the needs of seniors and raising the comfort and safety of their home living. The series of workshops involved researching lifestyles and user experiences of seniors, training research methods and tools, collaborations with furniture companies, and redesigning and upgrading existing furniture designs to the needs and preferences of seniors. The participants also developed information, communication, and exhibition design projects in relation to products, spaces, and messages for and about seniors.

In the period 2016–19 seven student workshops were organized: four in Riga, Latvia, two in Tallinn, Estonia, and one in Poznan, Poland. In addition, the BaltSe@nioR Innovation Camp 2018 was organized at the VIA University College in Herning, Denmark, a workshop in which students and companies worked closely together on new concepts and business models. The outcomes of the workshops were presented to partner companies as well as at DREMA Fair 2017 in Poznan and the Stockholm Furniture and Light Fair 2019.

The Art Academy of Latvia was the responsible project partner for organizing the creative design workshops with students. The BaltSe@nioR Innovation Camp was organized by the Development Centre UMT, the secretariat of Lifestyle & Design Cluster, a non-profit Innovation Cluster under the Danish Ministry of Higher Education and Science.

Results of the workshops can be found in the BaltSe@nioR Virtual Library (login required): https://baltsenior.com/profile-page/?id=5b84e68c-0e1d-44e2-94cc-d15e5889ffe9

Innovation Camp – a concentrated, cross-disciplinary development process

What is an Innovation Camp?

An Innovation Camp is a concentrated, cross-disciplinary development process where both students and companies work together using design thinking to develop new solutions to a given well-described problem – a solution that focuses on both a new concept and a new business model.

Purpose of the Innovation Camp

The purpose of the camp was to use Design Thinking methods to integrate design and business and in joint teams collaborate to come up with new sustainable products (furniture and interior) and business models that better support and meet seniors' needs in remaining autonomous in their own homes.

A further aim was to raise awareness among young designers and furniture constructors concerning requirements of the successful process of designing for seniors but also the needs seniors have and how to design products to fulfil them.

New working methods

The innovation camp was organized to introduce new working methods for product design to both students and companies and to stimulate and enhance collaboration between design students and companies across nationalities and competences, and to understand each others' working areas.

They were introduced to, and tried working hands-on with several methods and tools:

Basadur, Design thinking method cards, Business Model Canvas, Virtual Room, Virtual Library, user involved design and personas. Their work was based on information about seniors, sustainability etc. from different relevant experts. During the 5 days, they used the knowledge and tools in real life during the product and business development process and the results were three product suggestions to enhance elderly people's autonomy and wellbeing in their own home.

Match of teams:

Design teams were matched across nationalities, competences, experience and genders to ensure three equally competent and experienced teams. They were at day one matched with company team to set a very realistic task for the teams to pursue: Their products should be possible for a real company to produce and sell and should have a viable business model.

Participants:

Altogether 17 students, 10 companies, 7 teachers, 5 journalists and 14 project partners and 4 seniors from 6 countries participated during the 5 days of the BaltSe@nioR Innovation Camp.

Process:

Day 1: After introduction to the Innovation Camp concept and process the participants received expert input from:

1. Aske Juul Larsen, ethnologist at University of Copenhagen, Ph.D. in active aging and member of the Danish Government's new think tank regarding elderly people.

2. Anders Haahr – consultant and expert in implementation of the UN's 17 sustainable development goals.

3. Introduction to IDEO design thinking method.

4. Afterwards teambuilding and introduction to design brief for students. Companies also had a team building and match making session and introduction to Business Model Canvas and case presentation by one of the companies.

Day 2: In the morning: work in groups with the tasks and students had an introduction to Business Model Canvas in order to be able to also understand the business model related to the concept they developed.

After lunch again expert input:

1. Introduction to sustainability and circular economy by Henriette Melchiorsen, Development Centre UMT

2. Introduction to Virtual Room – and motion sensors by Pamela Ruiz Castro, University of Skövde

3. Introduction to use of workshops for prototypes and work in teams.

Day 3: Integrating circular economy into business models and test early prototypes and concept with invited seniors to check if concepts were viable for the target group

Halfway evaluation of all teams and check out with companies in the teams. (Companies were travelling home)

Adjusting concepts after midway evaluation.

Day 4: Prototyping and finishing concepts and presentations

Day 5: Build up presentations and give presentation of concepts and prototypes to an external jury of two design experts with in-depth knowledge about design for seniors.

Final presentation of winning team and press coverage.

Outcome:

The outcome was three very different concepts, which were all relevant for the target group, were realistic to be produced, all had a well-worked through business model.

Furthermore, students got new networks, insights into how other students from other countries work, all participants received expert knowledge about seniors, and tried out several new working methods, and got a good insight into what it means to works with real companies.

Companies also acquired expert knowledge about the growing target group of seniors, their needs and how to make products that better meet these new potential customers' needs.

Companies also were introduced to and tried hands on to work with several new tools and methods and got solid experience of what designers can do for their companies and how new collaborations can improve and strengthen their businesses.

Below follows an overview of all workshops and activities in chronological order:

Workshop No. 1 Design for active living and redesigning furniture

Riga, Latvia

7–10 November 2016

Participants

- 14 students and 4 tutors from the Art Academy of Latvia

- 6 students and 2 tutors from Poznan University of Life Sciences

- 7 students and 2 tutors from Tallinn University of Technology

Activities

The first workshop was dedicated to research and case studies on the lifestyles of seniors as well as the redesign of existing furniture products in collaboration with the award-winning furniture company Riga Chair. The workshop was divided into two parts: warming up with research activities and case studies and learning by doing in collaboration with industry. The teams focussed on the ageing process of the body and mind and how to retain an active and healthy lifestyle through fitness activities in the gym, at home, or at work.

Each morning the workshop opened with inspirational lectures in which stereotypes around seniors and ageing were challenged. The lectures were delivered by a rock musician, a fashion designer and a participant of a rowing expedition who recounted a boat trip to Rio. The participants were inspired and invigorated by great minds of various disciplines, including a social anthropologist, a digital architect and the chairperson of the Latvian fitness and healthcare development association LFVVNA. The rest of the day was spent on design workshops which concluded with an exhibition of the developed products and projects.

Methods

Furniture designers and manufacturers can take different approaches to redesigning furniture in order to serve the growing senior market segment and utilize opportunities for innovation. A practical approach is to take an existing furniture design as a basis and adapt certain of its features to the needs and preferences of seniors. Going beyond adapting features, conceptual and experimental approaches can be employed to translate existing design ideas or to explore new functions and products. Various other methods were used by the different teams depending on their specific projects: shadowing, interviews, data research on active living, etc.

Outcomes

Three teams focused on the redesign of an existing furniture product from the catalogue of the furniture company Riga Chair. Each team took a different approach to redesigning furniture and developed and tested their prototype. Other teams developed apps and accessories to make daily living for seniors more comfortable. Some of the projects were presented to experts from industry.

Workshop No. 2 Elderly on the Go

Tallinn, Estonia

27 February – 3 March 2017

Participants

- 8 students and 2 tutors from the Art Academy of Latvia

- 6 students and 2 tutors from Poznan University of Life Sciences

- 6 students and 4 tutors from Tallinn University of Technology

Activities

The aim of the second BaltSe@nioR workshop was to explore design possibilities through systematic visualized mapping. Two tasks were given to the participants in advance, to be prepared for the workshop. The first task was to shadow an elderly person (70+ years of age) with the method POEMS: Studying people, objects, environments, messages, and services in a context. Student team (two members) should agree with an elderly person for a shadowing session. The task is to observe how the shadowed person is getting ready, is going out, is on the way to shopping, visiting a doctor or friend and is getting back home. The observation should include the preparations for going out and getting back home including taking off the coat, putting away the shopping bag, etc. The whole observation should be documented by photos and field notes. After the field visit an analysis should be made by putting together the field notes and photos. For the analysis use the given template Elderly on the go, which is developed from the method POEMS.

The second task was studying the representation of elderly in the media. Identify 12 articles or media news on any kind of topics or issues related to elderly from your local mass media journals from the period of the last 4 weeks. Fill in the given template "Representation of elderly in media".

The four-day workshop started with introductory lectures by Beata Fabisiak (on BaltSe@nioR), Kai Saks (on the well-being of the elderly), Martin Pärn and Ruth-Helene Melioranski (on mapping), Adrian Paulsen (on systems-oriented design and gigamapping), and Rauno Pello (on service design and visualisation in practice).

Methods

Mapping is a long-established method to explore and organize complexities by graphically representing the elements and relations that are part of a complexity. Coined in 2009 by Prof Birger Sevaldson of the Oslo School of Architecture and Design, Gigamapping is 'super extensive mapping across multiple layers and scales with the goal of investigating relations between seemingly separate categories, hence providing boundary critiques on the conception and framing of systems.

Gigamapping is aimed at orienting in 'super-complexities' posed by our modern world. It is a technique of systems-oriented design and is based on systems thinking, design thinking, and visual thinking. Gigamaps lay out vast amounts of information and interconnections gathered from different sources, covering a wide and diverse spectrum of topics, and spanning macro and micro levels. The amount and diversity of elements and interconnections result in a 'myriadic quality' that provides 'an overall feel of the complexity of the system'.

Outcomes

During the workshop students trained with the different research methods and tools in practice to support research on the lifestyles and needs of seniors and topics related to population ageing. For instance, gigamapping was used to explore the topic of mobility issues in relation to the everyday activities of elderly.

Workshop No. 3 Designing information and spaces

Riga, Latvia

13–16 June 2017

Participants

- 11 students and 3 tutors from the Art Academy of Latvia

- 6 students from the BA School of Business and Finance

Activities

The information design workshop was implemented with the aim of informing industries about the new coming challenge of the ageing population and finding the best way how to support them with useful data.

During the creative design workshop functional design and graphic design students from the Design Department of the Art Academy of Latvia and students from the BA School of Business and Finance worked in interdisciplinary teams in cooperation with the bath company PAA and the furniture company Nakts mebeles as well as with a museum and providers of educational services to focus on the potential market audience and design methods which could be used to reach the audience and develop new products to improve the life quality of seniors. The workshop was led by the information design expert Martin Foessleitner.

Methods

Having an ageing population raises questions on how to make the buildings and spaces of institutions more attractive and accessible for a growing proportion of senior citizens, clients, and customers. This requires a deeper understanding of the needs and preferences of seniors and a holistic approach to the (re)design of spaces. The project presented in this document proposes the development of institution-specific design guidelines for both staff and external industry partners on such aspects as service, information, interaction, graphic, interior, and lighting design.

Outcomes

During this workshop four projects were developed representing four approaches to reach the industry – designers and producers of furniture, interior designers of public spaces (museums, educational institutions, etc.). This example presents a case study for a museum in Riga, Latvia.

Workshop No. 4 Furniture Factory Live at DREMA Fair 2017 Poznan

Poznan, Poland

11–15 September 2017

Participants

- 6 students and 3 tutors from the Art Academy of Latvia
- 27 students and 7 tutors from Poznan University of Life Sciences
- 4 students and 2 tutors from Tallinn University of Technology
- 1 student from the Technical University of Munich
- 2 students from the Norwegian University of Science and Technology

Activities

The workshop was organized parallel with DREMA Fair that took place at the Poznan International Fair. During this fair a full-scale furniture plant was built in one of the halls of the fairs and real production of furniture was performed. The event was called Furniture Factory LIVE. At the same time, design workshops at Poznan University of Life Sciences were organized. During that activity more craft works were performed.

The international group of participants designed furniture for children and seniors, developed their design and production technology and produced them live during the event. In addition, they redesigned Polish armchairs from the 1970s, adapting them to the needs of modern seniors. Forty-one students from Poland, Latvia, Estonia, Germany and Norway produced more than 50 pieces of furniture during 4 days of the event. As many as ten sets of children's furniture (beds with mattresses, desks, boxes and wardrobes) and five sets of furniture for seniors – beds with electric tilt adjustment, night cabinets and two wardrobes with special hangers for senior citizens – were manufactured. The furniture was next delivered to two selected orphanage homes and one senior home. The event was organized with the cooperation of the Poznan International Fair and the support of almost 30 companies. Moreover, during the redesign workshops 4 armchairs were created including one prototype of smart furniture.

Methods

Furniture may have a long lifespan and even outlive its owners. It may also be deeply integrated into the daily lives of its ageing users, both practically and emotionally. A way of responding to the changing needs and preferences of seniors is by upgrading old furniture instead of replacing it. Upgrading old furniture offers opportunities for innovative and sustainable approaches that combine raising comfort and safety as well as prolonging the lifespan of furniture and the emotional connection of users with their living environment.

Outcomes

During this workshop five projects were developed representing five approaches to upgrading old furniture, including upgrading basic product features, adding new functions, and integrating new technologies.

Students working during the Furniture Factory Live at DREMA Fair 2017 Poznan; Publicity photos by Art Academy Latvia

Workshop No. 5 Informing industry

Riga, Latvia

6–9 November 2017

Participants

- 14 students and 9 tutors from the Art Academy of Latvia

- 6 students and 2 tutors from Poznan University of Life Sciences

- 4 students and 2 tutors from Tallinn University of Technology

Activities

During the workshop students were supported with different tools to provide the information for the furniture companies regarding the upcoming challenge of the aging society and the profile of the future customer. There were very short inspirational talks of experts from storytelling, graphic, info, and UX design fields. That was immediately continued by practical working sessions in the above-mentioned fields. At the conclusion of the workshop, the whole story was put on Manual Mockup, using different languages (digital, printed, 3D) according to the students' proposals, based on what and where the furniture producers could receive and use newly created information. During the final presentation groups of students pitched their ideas and received feedback and criticism from industrialists and an expert of economics.

Methods

Furniture producers and other enterprises in product development are presented with both challenges and opportunities due to ageing populations. A way to adapt is to develop new design and business strategies based on research that maps current as well as future needs and preferences of this customer segment in relation to the enterprise's products, customer services, branding, and communication.

Outcomes

During the workshop five projects were developed representing five approaches of how to assist the industry in developing new strategies concerning the aging society.

One project presents a manual prepared for Riga Chair Factory, an award-winning furniture producer based in Latvia. It focuses on the needs of future visitors of large-scale public buildings such as theatres, concert halls, conference venues, libraries, and educational institutions, and the challenges posed to planning and designing auditorium seating. The aim of the manual is to support Riga Chair Factory, its clients, and partners in designing user friendly environments that take into account the needs and preferences of ageing audiences.

Another project presents a manual prepared for Kampenuss, a furniture and high-quality wood products producer based in Latvia. It focuses on the integration of the topic of the ageing population not only into produce development, but also in the company culture, branding, and communication.

The aim of the manual is to provide Kampenuss, its clients, and partners with a brand book and manual that serves as a tool to raise social awareness and responsibility through storytelling and actions.

Workshop No. 6 Seniors: understanding user experience

Tallinn, Estonia

19-22 February 2018

Participants

- 7 students and 2 tutors from the Art Academy of Latvia
- 4 students and 2 tutors from Poznan University of Life Sciences
- 6 students and 3 tutors from Tallinn University of Technology

Students working during the workshop in Tallinn in Feb 2018; Publicity photo by Art Academy Latvia

Activities

Understanding user experience has become a central, distinguishing feature of the best product development. This workshop focused on user experience for the elderly in their interaction with products and services. The object of the study was user experience in daily activities of the elderly. The goal of the workshop was to learn how to conduct user experience research that focused on the wholeness of experience, taking into consideration all aspects of user experience in complex situations. This included not only practical experience, but also intellectual or cognitive and emotional experiences that influence the kinds of interactions that take place in day care facilities. The workshop was supervised by Kaja Tooming Buchanan, PhD.

Methods

The learning objective was to explore the methods by which designers come to understand user needs, feelings, expectations and values. These methods are a preparation for developing breakthrough products – tangible and intangible – as well as interactions and services. For example, the students learned how to interpret needs, identify issues, visualize information, and generate ideas. During the workshop qualitative research was executed, including observations at the shopping mall. Topics such as experience, empathy, people-to-people interaction, people-to-environment interaction, and places of invention and discovery were discussed.

Outcomes

The deliverables of this workshop are student reports demonstrating their research and conclusions. The reports are digital and oral presentations.

BaltSe@nioR Innovation Camp

Herning, Denmark

2–6 July 2018

Participants

17 students, 10 companies, 7 teachers, 5 journalists and 14 project partners and 4 seniors from 6 partner countries

Activities

An Innovation Camp is a concentrated, cross-disciplinary development process where both students and companies work together using design thinking to develop new solutions to a given well-described problem – a solution that focuses on both a new concept and a new business model.

The purpose of the camp was to, via design thinking methods, integrate design and business and in joint teams collaborate to devise new sustainable products (furniture and interior) and business models that better support and meet seniors' needs in remaining autonomous in their own homes.

Another aim was to raise awareness among young designers and furniture constructors concerning requirements of the successful process of designing for seniors but also the needs seniors have and how to design products to fulfil them.

Methods

The innovation camp was organized to introduce new working methods for product design to both students and companies and to stimulate and enhance collaboration between design students and companies across nationalities and competences, and to understand each other's working areas.

They were introduced to and tried working hands-on with several methods and tools: Basadur, Design thinking method cards, Business Model Canvas, Virtual Room, Virtual Library, user involved design and personas. Their work was based on information about seniors, sustainability, etc., from different relevant experts. During the five days, they used the knowledge and tools in real life during the product and business development process and the results were three product suggestions to enhance elderly people's autonomy and wellbeing in their own home.

Design teams were matched across nationalities, competences, experience and genders to ensure three equally competent and experienced teams. They were at day one matched with each company team to set a very realistic task for the teams to pursue: their products should be possible for a real company to produce and sell and have a viable business model.

Outcomes

The outcome was three very different concepts, which were all relevant for the target group, were realistic to produce, and all had a well-worked-through business model. Furthermore, the student built new networks, gained insights into how other students from other countries work, and all participants received expert knowledge about seniors, tried out several new working methods, and obtained a good insight into what it means to work with real companies.

Companies also acquired expert knowledge about the growing target group of seniors, their needs and how to make products that better meet these new potential customers' needs. Companies also were introduced to and tried hands on to work with several new tools and methods and got solid experience of what designers can do for their companies and how new collaborations can improve and strengthen their businesses.

Workshop No. 7 Greenhouse Exhibition at the Stockholm Furniture and Light Fair 2019

Riga, Latvia

27–30 November 2018

Participants

- 10 students and 4 tutors from the Art Academy of Latvia

- 6 students and 2 tutors from Poznan University of Life Sciences

- 3 students and 2 tutors from Tallinn University of Technology

Activities

The main challenge of the workshop was to prepare the common concept of the exhibition at the Stockholm Furniture and Light fair Greenhouse section in February 2019. Three universities – the Art Academy of Latvia, Poznan University of Life Sciences and Tallinn University of Technology – and their collaboration within the project BaltSe@nioR is going to be exhibited in the Stockholm Furniture and Light fair Greenhouse section in February 2019. The purpose of the participation of three partner universities in the Stockholm Furniture and Light fair is to reach out to a Scandinavian audience in an effective and personal manner. By putting up a stall in the Greenhouse exhibition, the Art Academy of Latvia, Poznan University of Life Sciences and Tallinn University of Technology also would like to give our design students and their product prototypes visibility and publicity.

Before the workshop it was agreed to exhibit nine projects (three from each university) created in collaboration with local furniture producers. During the autumn study semester students from all three universities conducted research about the needs and demands of the elderly, defined problems and worked in collaboration with one local furniture producer to introduce a solution.

Methods

During the workshop students were supported with different tools to develop the message – strategy and communication, and exhibition stand concept and design.

There were very short inspirational talks of experts from branding, strategy, communication and experience in design. After the input of each expert the workshop was continued by practical working. Students worked in small groups and at the conclusion of the workshop the whole story was told with the help of a developed scale model and well-prepared verbal communication.

The main issues students were trained on during the workshop were:

- How to define the message students will communicate in the Stockholm Furniture and Light fair?

- How to express their message to the target group?

- How to attract attention to the message?

- How to start a continuous dialogue between students and visitors?

- How to find the best way to tell the story?

Outcomes

The outcome was two very different concepts for the Stockholm Furniture and Light fair Greenhouse section in February 2019. The concept "Super Power" was the one chosen to develop to implement. Time doesn't stop for anyone. There may arrive a moment when each of us would need a Super Power, which would provide us with quality of life equal to that of our fellow people. With the concept of the exhibition stand and the developed design products we want to draw the attention of furniture producers to the fact that society is ageing, and it needs specially adjusted products which eliminate discomfort and improve our everyday quality of life. Let's help regain the Super Power!

Other publications by the Baltic Sea Academy

Volume 1

Strategies for the Development of Crafts and SMEs in the Baltic Sea Region 2011;

ISBN: 9783842326125

Volume 2

Strategy Programme for education policies in the Baltic Sea Region 2012 (2nd edition);

ISBN: 9783848252534

Volume 3

Education Policy Strategies today and tomorrow around the "Mare Balticum" 2011;

ISBN: 9783842374218

Volume 4

Energy Efficiency and Climate Protection around the "Mare Balticum" 2011;

ISBN: 9783844800982

Volume 5

SME relevant sectors in the BSR: Personnel organisation, Energy and Construction 2012;

ISBN: 9783848202577

Volume 6

Strategies and Promotion of Innovation in Regional Policies around the Mare Balticum 2012;

ISBN 9783848218295

Volume 7

Strategy Programme for innovation in regional policies in the Baltic Sea Region 2012;

ISBN: 9783848230471331

Volume 8

Humanity - Innovative economic development through human growth by Kenneth Daun 2012;

ISBN: 9783848253395

Volume 9

Economic Perspectives, Qualification and Labour Market Integration of Women in the Baltic Sea Region 2013;

ISBN: 9783732243952

Volume 10

Corporate Social Responsibility and Women's Entrepreneurship around the Mare Balticum 2013;

ISBN: 9783732278459

Volume 11

Development of the enterprises' competitiveness in the context of demographic challenges 2013;

ISBN: 973732293971

Volume 12

Age, Gender and Innovation – Strategy program and action plans for the Baltic Sea Region 2014;

ISBN: 9783735784919

Volume 13

Innovative SMEs by Gender and Age around the Mare Balticum 2014;

ISBN: 9783735791191

Volume 14

Innovation in SMEs, previous projects in the Baltic Sea Region and future needs 2014;

ISBN: 9783735791191 332

Volume 15

Building the socially responsible employment policy in the Baltic Sea Region 2014;

ISBN: 9783735790484

Volume 16

Women and elderly on the BSR labour market - good practices' analysis and transfer 2014;

ISBN: 9783735791412

Volume 17

Manual and Best Practices for innovative SMEs by Gender and Age in the Baltic Sea Region 2014;

ISBN: 9783735791405

Volume 18

Civilizational changes and the competitiveness of modern enterprises 2014;

ISBN: 9783732282449

Volume 19

Female Entrepreneurship – Evidence from Germany and the Baltic Sea Region and analysis of women's activity in SMEs in Poland 2014;

ISBN: 9783735757296

Volume 20

Manual for trainings and dual study courses of the sector skills alliance "Skills Energy BSR" 2015;

ISBN: 9783734750120

Volume 21

Work-based Learning around the Mare Balticum 2015;

ISBN: 9783734776151 333

Volume 22

The Hamburg Model – exemplary integration of youth into vocational education 2015;

ISBN: 978373863006

Volume 23

Improvement of Skills in the Green Economy through the Advanced Training Programs on Cradle to Cradle® 2016;

ISBN: 9783741276026

Volume 24

Qualification and Integration of young people by dual vocational training 2017;

ISBN 9783744888189

Volume 25

Common Vocational Training to Master craftsman in the Baltic Sea Region;
ISBN 9783752829013

Volume 26

Further Vocational Training Energy Service Manager;
ISBN 9783752854305

Volume 27

BaltSe@nior - Challenges and innovative solutions in product development for seniors' home living
ISBN 9783749456093

Members of the Hanse Parlament

Baltic Institute of Finland, Finland

Belarusian Chamber of Commerce and Industry, Belarus

Chamber of Craftsmanship and Enterprise in Bialystok, Poland

Chamber of Craft Region Kaliningrad, Russia

Chamber of Crafts and SME in Katowice, Poland

Chamber of Crafts in Opole, Poland

Chamber of Crafts and SME in Szczecin, Poland

Craft Chamber in Rzeszów, Poland

Dresden Chamber of Skilled Crafts and Small Businesses, Germany

Eastern Mecklenburg-Western Pomerania Chamber of Handicraft, Germany

Hamburg Chamber of Skilled Crafts and Small Businesses, Germany

Handicraft Chamber of Ukraine, Ukraine

Handicraft Chamber Leningrad Region, Russia

Handicraft and Small Business Chamber Lublin, Poland

Hungarian Association of Craftsmen Corporations, Hungary

IBC Innovationsfabrikken Kolding, Denmark

Kaliningrad Chamber of Commerce and Industry, Russia

Kontiki Vocational training company, Hungary

Kujawsko-Pomorska Chamber of Craft and SMEs, Poland

Kyiv Chamber of Commerce and Industry, Ukraine

Latvian Chamber of Crafts, Latvia

Latvian Chamber of Industry and Commerce, Latvia

Lower Silesian Chamber of Craft and Small and Medium-sized Businesses, Poland

Master of Crafts Norway, Norway

Nordic Forum of Crafts, Norway

Organisation of Handicraft Businesses in Trondheim, Norway

Panevezys Chamber of Commerce, Industry and Crafts, Lithuania

Pomeranian Chamber of Handicrafts for SMEs, Poland

Russian Chamber of Crafts, Russia

Schwerin Chamber of Skilled Crafts, Germany

Small Business Chamber Warsaw, Poland

Vilnius Chamber of Commerce, Industry and Crafts, Lithuania

Warmia and Mazury Chamber of Crafts and Small Business in Olsztyn, Poland

Wielkopolska Craft Chamber in Poznan, Poland

Association for the promotion of Hamburg's economic history and the tradition of the Hanseatic League, Germany

Eastern European Association of German Business e. V., Germany

Haus Rissen Hamburg, Germany

Initiative e. V. – Promotion Society for Protestant Responsibility in the Economy of Central and Eastern Europe, Germany

Marshal's Office of the Pomorskie Voivodship, Poland

Signal Iduna Gruppe, Germany

Włodzimierz Szordykowski (Honorary member), Poland

Members of the Baltic Sea Academy

Brest State Technical University, Belarus

Gdansk University of Technology, Poland

Hamburg Institute of International Economics, Germany

Hamburg University of Corporate Education, Germany

Hanseatic Institute for Support of Small and Medium Enterprises, Poland

Hanse Parlament e.V., Germany

International Business Academy, Denmark

Lithuanian University of Educational Sciences, Lithuania

Lund University, Sweden

Panevezys University of Applied Sciences, Lithuania

Saint-Petersburg State University of Economics, Russia

Satakunta University of Applied Sciences, Finland

Tampere University of Technology, Finland

University 21, Germany

University of Bialystok, Poland

University of Latvia, Latvia

VIA University College, Denmark

Vilnius Gediminas Technical University, Lithuania

Võru County Vocational Training Centre, Estonia